Embellishing with Beads

Beaded pillow
Fringed
Owned by Susan Ure

Embellishing
with Beads

Nancy Nehring

A Sterling/Chapelle Book

Sterling Publishing Co., Inc. New York

Chapelle, Ltd.:

Jo Packham
Sara Toliver
Cindy Stoeckl

Editor: Laura Best
Editorial Director: Caroll Shreeve
Art Director: Karla Haberstich
Copy Editor: Marilyn Goff
Graphics Illustrator: Kim Taylor
Staff: Burgundy Alleman, Areta Bingham, Ray Cornia,
         Emily Frandsen, Susan Jorgensen, Barbara Milburn,
         Lecia Monsen, Karmen Quinney, Desirée Wybrow

If you have any questions or comments, please contact:
Chapelle, Ltd., Inc., P.O. Box 9252, Ogden, UT 84409
(801) 621-2777 • (801) 621-2788 Fax
e-mail: chapelle@chapelleltd.com
web site: chapelleltd.com

Beaded purse
Owned by Susan Ure

Library of Congress Cataloging-in-Publication Data Available

Nehring, Nancy.
   Embellishing with beads / Nancy Nehring.
      p. cm.
   ISBN 1-4027-0059-8
   1. Beadwork. I. Title.
TT860.N44 2003
745.58'2--dc21
                                    2002154879

10 9 8 7 6 5 4 3 2 1

Published by Sterling Publishing Co., Inc.
387 Park Avenue South, New York, NY 10016
©2003 by Nancy Nehring
Distributed in Canada by Sterling Publishing
c/o Canadian Manda Group, One Atlantic Avenue, Suite 105
Toronto, Ontario, Canada M6K 3E7
Distributed in Great Britain by Chrysalis Books
64 Brewery Road, London N7 9NT, England
Distributed in Australia by Capricorn Link (Australia) Pty. Ltd.
P.O. Box 704, Windsor, NSW 2756, Australia
Printed in China
All Rights Reserved

Sterling ISBN 1-4027-0059-8

Introduction

Beads make spectacular embellishments for fashion, home-décor objects, and artwork. They call attention to a piece by adding interest, sparkle, texture, and movement. Beads suggest elegance and wealth because good quality beadwork is still hand-stitched and, therefore, quite expensive.

In the past, we lavished beadwork on special-occasion items. Bridal and evening wear were often adorned with intricate and artistic bead patterns. We still bead specialty items, but have expanded the craft to include all sorts of costumes, casual everyday wear such as jeans and T-shirts, and pillows for the sofa.

Stitching countless small beads is quite time consuming. A full-beaded couture evening dress can take up to 200 hours to bead and may weigh over 40 pounds. You may get by with a few less beads. Beads are rarely used alone. You can weave sequins, rhinestones, buttons, metal threads, ribbons, braids, and cords into your beaded creation. These related embellishments provide interest and focus against a backdrop of tiny beads. Using the techniques and suggestions in this book, you will learn to apply your beads quickly and efficiently. We will cover how to select the right types of beads for your projects, purchase needed supplies, prepare your fabrics, and develop and transfer your own beading patterns.

We will introduce the most-common techniques for adding embellishments to beadwork. The projects spotlighted in this book are used exclusively as examples. They are not meant to be duplicated but to excite your creativity with a multitude of colors and shapes to create your own masterpiece.

Don't sew? No problem. You can add beads to ready-to-wear garments and purchased home furnishings. We will tell you exactly what you need for each type of project. Enjoy!

Peruvian tassel belt
*Seed bead embellishments
and multicolored thread*
Owned by Susan Ure

Table of contents

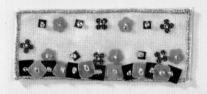

Beaded cards
Designed by Mei Fields
Saffron Cards

General information

Beading does not require a lot of supplies or equipment. Some fabric, a needle and thread, and beads will suffice for small projects. More items are, of course, necessary for larger projects. However, an enlightened choice of the materials you use will make your beading more pleasurable and the finished result more enjoyable.

Cost is rarely a factor with small beads because they are plentiful and inexpensive; however, large beads are sold individually and the cost can add up quickly.

If you find a bead you like, but the price is too high, see if you can find a similar bead in a lower quality or alternate material. As always, buy the best quality you can afford. You will be investing significant time into your beaded projects, so do not skimp by using less expensive materials than necessary.

Beaded tassel
*Seed bead embellishments
and multicolored thread*
Owned by Susan Ure

Assorted bead collage
Series 8" x 8"
Janet Hofacker

How many beads do I need?

The best way to determine how many beads you will need for a project is to buy a few of the beads you plan on using and make a sample swatch. Take a small piece of your project fabric and stitch on the desired beads and/or embellishments. For small beads, cover a 1" square at about the same density as your final design plan. For large beads, sew just a few onto a 1" square.

Large beads are sold individually. Count out how many you will need. Can you obtain enough beads? Not all beads are available in large quantities. Small beads are sold either by weight in plastic bags or tubes, or by the hank. A hank is 10 or more lengths of prestrung beads tied together. (See Figure 1)

To buy beads by weight, weigh the 1"-square beaded swatch on a postal scale. Then estimate how many square inches of beadwork you will work using that bead. Multiply to estimate the weight of beads you will need.

For beads in a hank, estimate the number of beads you will need by counting the beads in the 1"-square swatch. Estimate the number of square inches to be covered and multiply to get the total number needed. Hanks do not all have the same amount of beads. After you know how many you will need, count the number of beads on one strand of the hank and the number of strands in the hank. Multiply to estimate the number of beads in a hank. Then divide the total number of beads needed by the number of beads in a hank to estimate the number of hanks you will need.

Purchase more beads than you think you need to complete your project. If your local store does not have enough beads in stock, have the store order all of the beads you need from one dye lot. Do not expect to be able to go back and buy more beads to match ones you already have.

Figure 1

Figure 2

What should I know about bead origin?

Closely inspect the beads for type and quality. Ask the salesperson if you do not know what to look for. Materials often mimic each other but the durability of similar-looking materials may vary widely. For instance, glass and plastic pearls can look like the real thing, but the pearly finishes can flake off.

Check the hole size. Are you able to stitch the beads onto your swatch with the size of needle and type of thread you want to use? The size of the bead and the size of the bead hole affect how easy a bead is to work with. In some bead lots, the beads vary greatly in size. This works if you are randomly spacing your beads. However, if you want a solid look, the beads must be uniform.

As you gain experience, you will be able to make some guesses about availability and properties of a bead based on when and where it was manufactured. For example, many old styles of machine-cut faceted beads have been discontinued, so the supply may be limited to what you see in front of you. Or, modern Czech dyed beads may not be colorfast. It never hurts to ask the salesperson about where and when your beads were manufactured and how durable are their qualities. Beads can look as if they change colors in different types of lighting. For example, the same bead may not look the same under natural light as it does under florescent light. Colors can also fade or change when exposed to high heat or ultra-violet light. (See Figure 2)

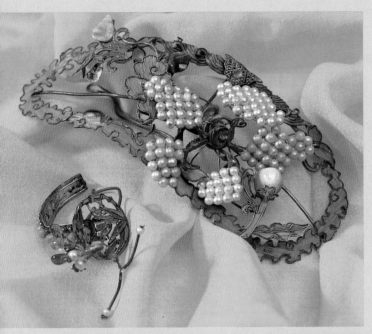

Antique Chinese hair clip & earrings
Embellished with butterfly wings
Owned by Susan Ure

Is the bead durable?

Beadwork does not handle cleaning or ironing well. If you are going to clean the finished project, clean your swatch in the same manner before beading. Washing may cause some finishes to flake off or change color, some dyes to fade or run, or some metals to tarnish. Dry-cleaning or ironing can cause beads to change colors, especially gold beads to silver. Cleaning and ironing may also melt plastics.

Consider the durability of your beads even for projects that will not be cleaned. For example, brass and sterling silver beads will tarnish with time. In general, plastic beads stand up to the hardest use. More fragile materials should be used in projects that will endure minimal use and cleaning.

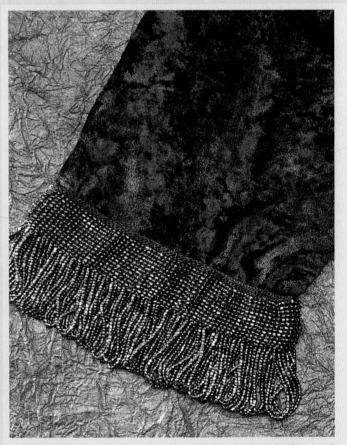

Beaded scarf
Fringed with bead dangles
Owned by Jo Packham

Bead qualities

It takes many little beads to make a big impression, and bead selection can be an overwhelming task. Knowing what types of beads are available and the reasons for choosing each one will help you select beads that add up to a great overall look. Remember, the general pattern is more important than any one individual bead.

Although you will find beads made from metal, bone, plastic, gemstones, or other materials, your primary work bead will be made of glass. Each bead type has a specific use based on size, shape, and its manner of reflecting light.

Beaded hat lamp shade
Various beads strung on copper wire
Owned by Susan Ure

Glass beads

All small beads (under 4mm), and most larger beads are made of glass. Glass beads come in over 2000 combinations when you consider their color, opacity, and finish. Color is usually the primary consideration when choosing beads; but shape, opacity, and finish, all affect the way light reflects off beads, influencing their overall look and appeal.

Glass beads are made in three differing degrees of opacity:

• opaque—a solid color that cannot be seen through.

• translucent—a diffused color which allows light through the center.

• transparent—clear or colored glass that is easy to see through.

Opaque glass is used when you need to hide the thread.

Translucent glass, also known as "greasy" or "Vaseline® glass" is usually only found in antique beads and lends an aged quality.

Transparent beads allow light to pass through them, giving life to the project. You will need to do a little more work with transparent beads to hide threads, but the end result is usually worth the effort.

Fiber-optic beads have fused-glass strands resembling a cat's eye.

Different colors or opacities can be combined in a single glass bead. Combining glass types is common on large lampwork beads.

Occasionally small beads are made with more than one glass type as well. Striped beads typically have a core of one color and narrow bands of a second color down the sides. White-heart beads have an opaque core (usually white or yellow) with an overlay of a second color (usually transparent blue or red). (See Figure 3)

Glass Types for Small Beads

opaque – solid color throughout, no light passes through

translucent – light passes through, hole indistinct

transparent – clear glass, light passes easily, hole visible

dyed – glass colored by dyeing

striped – glass core with stripes of second color

white heart – opaque core with overlay of transparent color

Hole Finishes (on transparent beads)

silver lined

gold lined

copper lined

color lined

Figure 3

Glass bead finishes

Finishes can be applied to transparent beads. The bead hole, the outer surface, or both can be finished. (See Figure 4)

The opaque linings covered by transparent glass give the beads the illusion of depth. The lining also hides the threads used to stitch the beads. Metallic linings add sparkle to beads and a metallic silver lining can be used

Figure 4

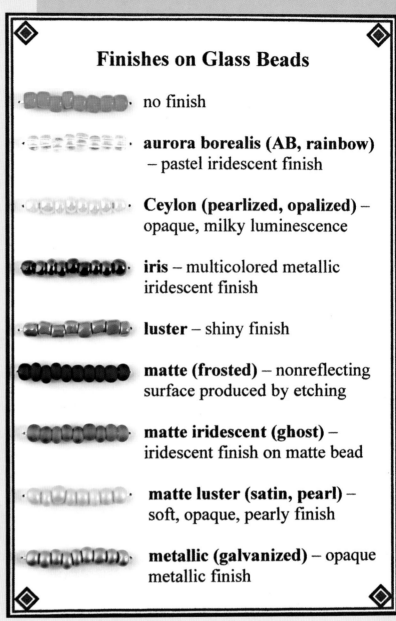

Figure 5

with all colors. Clear beads are often finished with silver, copper, or gold linings for a metallic look. Adding a colored lining to a clear bead produces the same overall effect. When selecting finishes, consider how they modify the light reflectance, color, and opacity of the beads. Traditional finishes for glass beads are shown in Figure 5.

Metal beads

Several different metals are used for beads. Gold beads have a warm, rich look. Gold beads (14k and 18k) are expensive, but gold-plated and gold-filled beads give much the same look for a lower price. Sterling silver provides beads with a rich silver color, which eventually tarnishes, giving an antique look. Nickel-plated metal is your choice if you want your beads to stay bright silver indefinitely.

Less expensive metals such as brass, bronze, and copper may be lacquered to keep them shiny. Anodized aluminum or niobium produces beads in a wide range of bright metallic colors. Metal beads with grooves or faces sparkle nearly as much as glass. (See Figure 6)

Many Victorian-period tassels, lamp shades, and handbags were embellished with fancy metal beads. Antique beadwork from India during the same period has textured-metal beadwork, often with tiny mirrors.

Figure 6

15

Natural-material beads

Natural materials have been used for beads since our ancestors strung their first necklaces. Beads from natural materials can be divided into two groups: shiny and expensive such as gemstones and pearls, and earthy with a matte finish such as wood, shell, and bone. (See Figure 7)

Precious and semiprecious gemstones are still treasured and do not need to be outrageously expensive. The freshwater pearls, known as "rice crispies," are affordable enough to use en masse. For the budget conscious, earthy beads have always been a good choice.

The hallmark of ethnic beadwork, beads are made from materials as dissimilar as shells, wood, amber, bones, animal teeth, and seeds. Most natural-material beads were originally created by native peoples and are strongly associated with an ethnic look.

Bead necklace
Strung with fancy beads
Owned by Jo Packham

Figure 7

16

Nonglass beads

Modern technology has brought some enticing new offerings to the bead table. Florescent and glow-in-the-dark beads are available to put finishing touches on jeans and other sorts of everyday wear. Polymer clay is now used extensively to make "picture" beads that imitate millefiori, stone, shell cameos, and nearly every other type of bead material. Do not forget to experiment with the new plastic "miracle" beads—inexpensive imitations of otherwise costly beads, they have a deep lustrous glow and can look stunning.

Plastic beads

Plastic is the most versatile material for beads. It is used to create lightweight beads, beads with intricate or realistic shapes, and beads that mimic other materials for less cost. For large beads, where the weight of glass can tear the fabric or make the completed garment too heavy to wear, plastic beads are perfect. Plastic can be molded into intricate designs such as miniature leaves, and realistic shapes such as fruits and animals. Also plastic beads and other embellishments come in myriad colors. (See Figure 8)

Figure 8

Bead sizes & shapes

Seed beads

Seed beads are the most commonly used beads in colorful, complex designs. Seed beads are small, donut-shaped, glass beads cut from glass canes (long tubes of glass), then rounded and polished by tumbling in hot sand. (See Figure 9)

Seed beads are also known by the French term *"rocailles."* Each bead reflects a single point of light, so a number of beads is needed to make fabric shimmer. Seed beads are available in every color and finish.

Common sizes for seed beads range from 15° (fifteen aught) to 5°. The larger the size number, the smaller the bead. Roughly correlate the bead size to the number of beads required to cover 15mm (⅝"). For example, it would take approximately eleven 11° beads to cover ⅝" of fabric. Size 11° comes in the most finishes and colors and is, therefore, the most frequently used.

Three variations of seed beads deserve mention: true-cut, square-hole, and fringe beads. A true-cut bead has one flat (cut) face, as shown magnified in Figure 10 on page 19.

Occasionally, a true-cut will have two flat faces. In a mass of beads, light catches on the cut faces and is reflected.

Square-hole beads have flat surfaces in the hole that reflect the light so the beads sparkle.

Fringe (or drop) beads are a recent creation. A seed bead formed with an off-center hole, these beads work well as the terminating bead.

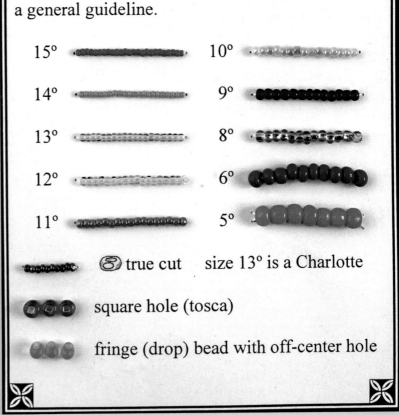

Seed Beads (Rocailles)

Small donut-shaped beads cut from glass cane and polished by tumbling in hot sand. Common sizes are 15° to 5°. The size is approx. the number of beads in 15mm (⅝"), i.e. there are 11 beads in 15mm for size 11° beads. Manufacturers do not size beads precisely so sizing can only be used as a general guideline.

15°	10°
14°	9°
13°	8°
12°	6°
11°	5°

true cut   size 13° is a Charlotte

square hole (tosca)

fringe (drop) bead with off-center hole

Figure 9

Small faceted beads

Small faceted beads are seed beads with multiple flat faces. (See Figure 13) Like their donut-shaped cousins, these beads are used en masse. But, whereas a donut-shaped bead reflects one point of light, a faceted bead reflects multiple points of light, bringing more sparkle.

Small faceted beads are cut from hexagonal-shaped glass cane. They are polished by heating up the cut beads near their melting point, which causes the edges to contract and become smooth. The 2-cut and 3-cut beads were the only styles made from shaped cane when glass was worked by hand. In a 2-cut bead, cane is simply cut into short lengths and polished. (See Figure 11) The 3-cut bead has additional facets on each end of the bead. (See Figure 12)

Today, with the mechanized methods of glassmaking, small faceted beads from several shapes of cane are possible. The square hexagon-cane is used as well as pentagon-, rectangle-, and triangle-shaped canes. Each shape reflects light differently and gives off a different appearance.

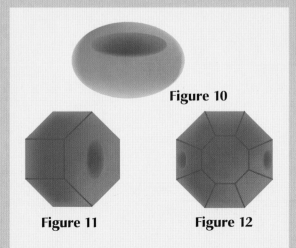

Figure 10

Figure 11   **Figure 12**

Small Faceted (Cut) Beads

Faceted beads are glass beads with flat faces. 2-cut and 3-cut beads are used en masse like seed beads. Facets are from the flat faces on hexagonal cane used to make the beads. These beads are also called cut beads or H (for hexagonal) beads. Beads that are square (flat) on the ends are called 2-cut. 2-cuts are the same as #1 bugle beads except 2-cuts are polished. If the cut ends are also faceted, the beads are called 3-cut. Sizes 13° to 8° are available.

2-Cut 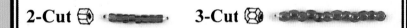 **3-Cut**

Shaped Canes   other shapes of cane in sizes up to 4mm diameter are used to make beads.

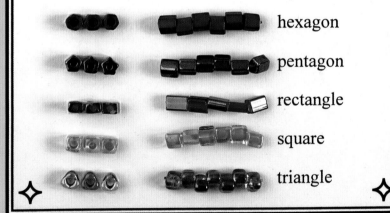

hexagon

pentagon

rectangle

square

triangle

Figure 13

The size range of small faceted beads is limited. Today, 2-cut and 3-cut beads are only made in sizes 12°–9°. A size 11° 2-cut bead can be easily confused with a size 1 hexagonal bugle bead. The only difference is that the double-cut is polished and the bugle is not. Other shaped-cane beads can be as large as 4mm. Large faceted beads 3mm and larger are easier to make by other methods.

Large faceted beads

Large faceted beads are 3mm or larger with multiple flat faces designed to reflect light from many angles. These beads are used individually or in small groups to focus attention. They can be machine-cut, hand-cut, or molded from individual pieces of glass. Machine-cut beads are the most uniform. Hand-cut beads often have irregular facets and, sometimes, cut marks on the facets. Molded beads are fire-polished to remove mold marks, but this process also rounds the edges. You can distinguish cut beads from molded beads by looking at the angles where the facets meet. Cut beads will have sharp angles, molded beads are rounded. (See Figure 14)

Round beads range from 3mm to 10mm in 1mm increments. Larger sizes increase by 2mm increments. This extensive size range was developed for necklaces composed of graduated beads. Sizes over 10mm have limited use in beading on fabric because the weight of is so heavy. Beads above 10mm are usually substituted with flat-backed stones.

Other shapes are made in faceted beads with cube, cone, drop, and cathedral being the most common. There is a constant turnover of shapes or number of facets used as old styles are discontinued and new styles are introduced.

Faceted beads larger than 6mm are also made of plastic and metal. The quality of faceted plastic beads varies greatly. Plastic beads made for children's crafts are poorly formed and do not reflect light. They are not appropriate for use in serious beadwork. Faceted metal beads are often hollow and are, therefore, very lightweight.

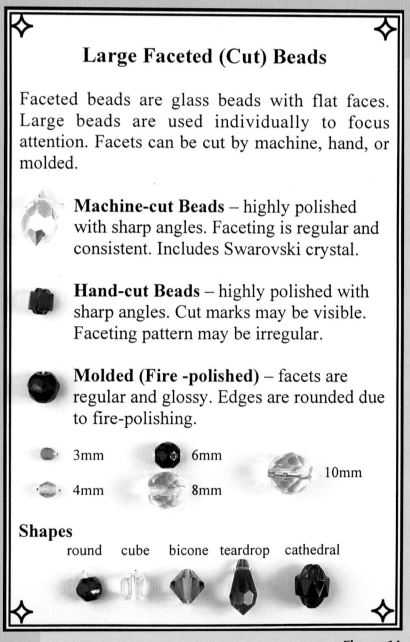

Large Faceted (Cut) Beads

Faceted beads are glass beads with flat faces. Large beads are used individually to focus attention. Facets can be cut by machine, hand, or molded.

Machine-cut Beads – highly polished with sharp angles. Faceting is regular and consistent. Includes Swarovski crystal.

Hand-cut Beads – highly polished with sharp angles. Cut marks may be visible. Faceting pattern may be irregular.

Molded (Fire -polished) – facets are regular and glossy. Edges are rounded due to fire-polishing.

3mm   6mm   10mm

4mm   8mm

Shapes

round   cube   bicone   teardrop   cathedral

Figure 14

Bugle beads

Bugle beads are long tubular beads made from glass cane with a round or hexagonal cross section, the same cane used for seed beads. For added sparkle, bugles may have silver linings or hexagonal bugles may be twisted. Although bugle beads come in the same colors and finishes as seed beads, you will find that silver-lined bugle beads are the most popular.

Because of their length, bugle beads draw the eye along their length and focus attention. They are frequently used in fringes to create a dangling effect.

Be careful when handling bugle beads as the ends are not polished and are quite sharp. Thread used to sew or string bugle beads should be heavily waxed to protect it from being cut by the edge of the bead.

Often grouped with bugle beads are maco tubes. Maco tubes are tiny glass tubular beads of recent design. They are 1mm in diameter and 1mm, 2mm, or 4mm in length. They are a smaller version of the bugle bead. The colors and finishes available for maco tubes are limited. (See Figure 15)

Although maco tubes are made of glass, metal tube beads are also available. Gold-plated and sterling silver tube beads, called liquid gold and liquid silver respectively, have either square (flat) ends or rounded ends. Metal tube beads also come in less expensive metals such as brass.

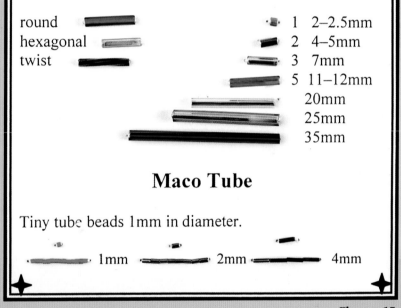

Bugle Beads

Long, tubular beads cut from round or hexagonal glass cane with unpolished, straight ends.

Two size systems are used. The number system, from $^1/_2$ to 5, is the length of that number of 11° seed beads. For instance, a #3 is the same length as three 11° seed beads. Bugle beads are also sized in mm. Common lengths are 2mm to 35mm, but lengths down to 1mm and up to 50mm can be found. Bugle beads are the same diameter as an 11° seed bead.

round
hexagonal
twist

1   2–2.5mm
2   4–5mm
3   7mm
5   11–12mm
    20mm
    25mm
    35mm

Maco Tube

Tiny tube beads 1mm in diameter.

1mm   2mm   4mm

Figure 15

Drops

Drops, also called pendants and dangles, are attached at one end of the bead instead of in the center. (See Figure 16) Drops swing freely, adding movement to the beadwork. The name "drop" comes from teardrop, the most common drop shape. Other classic drop shapes include daggers, crystals, and fringe (seed) beads with offset centers. The most intriguing drops are formed into fanciful and realistic shapes—veined leaves, seashells, and tiny bell drops.

Drops come in sizes varying from minute fringe beads to beads designed specifically for jewelry that are too large and heavy for fabric. Most drops have a hole running vertically or horizontally through the bead. (See Figure 17) Some drops have an embedded wire or are mounted in a bead cap. Other beads can be made into drops by passing a T-pin through a bead and then making a loop in the tip.

A variety of materials are used for drops. Most glass drops are molded, but cut drops are also available. Fanciful- and realistic-shaped drops are usually plastic or metal, because glass is too fragile for intricate shapes. Good quality, lightweight plastic is used for larger drops. Plastic beads are often finished to match the finishes used on glass beads. Natural materials such as seashells or crystals are sometimes mounted whole and used as drops. Drop beads also include a wide variety of brass and sterling silver charms.

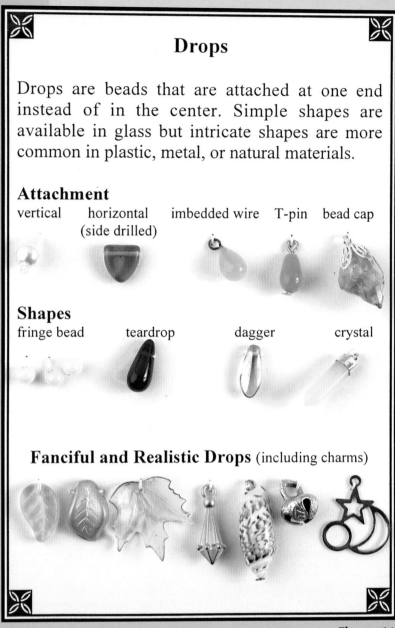

Drops

Drops are beads that are attached at one end instead of in the center. Simple shapes are available in glass but intricate shapes are more common in plastic, metal, or natural materials.

Attachment

vertical   horizontal   imbedded wire   T-pin   bead cap
(side drilled)

Shapes

fringe bead   teardrop   dagger   crystal

Fanciful and Realistic Drops (including charms)

Figure 16

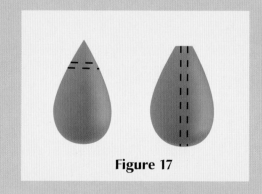

Figure 17

Fancy beads

Fancy beads are large decorative beads used for accent. As accents, these are only used in pieces that will be viewed close-up where they add considerable interest to a design.

Although sometimes made of glass, fancy beads are more often made of materials that provide textural interest and are lighter in weight. (See Figure 18) Plastic and metal beads can be formed into beads with intricate shapes and fine detail. These beads may be surface-decorated with piercings, inset jewels, or enamel.

Beads from natural materials include gemstones, pearls, shell, bone, and wood. Gemstones and pearls are used on the most expensive embroideries.

Fancy beads are often used to embellish handmade stuffed toys and dolls. They are popular choices as an option to pretty buttons on handiwork, such as knitting and crocheting.

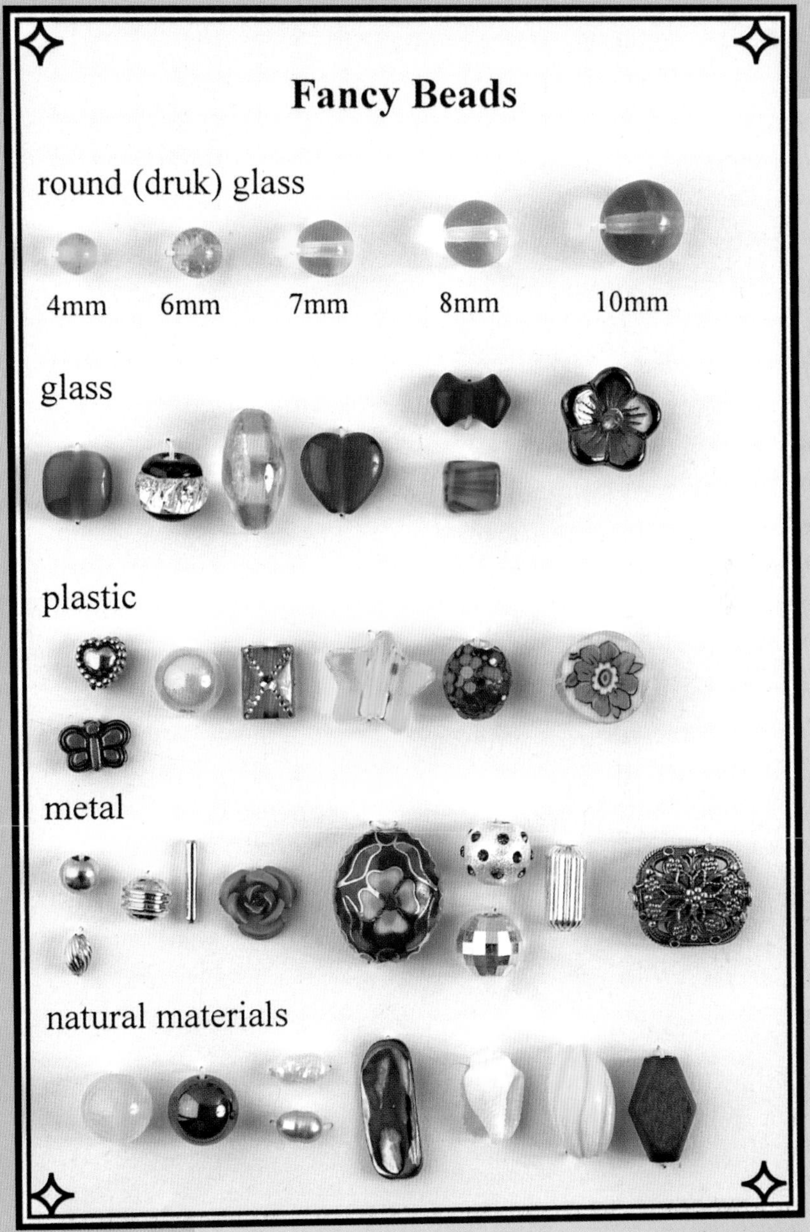

Fancy Beads

round (druk) glass

4mm 6mm 7mm 8mm 10mm

glass

plastic

metal

natural materials

Figure 18

Fabrics

You see fabrics from the finest chiffons to the heaviest velvets embellished with beads. You can use any fabric for your outer fashion fabric if you choose appropriate beads and reinforce the fabric as necessary. Beadwork is hard on fabric. Beading adds a lot of weight, affects the drape, and may even distort the weave, especially on the bias. The threads used to stitch the beads in place reduce the flex and stretch of a fabric. Beading causes fabric to "shrink" up to $\frac{1}{16}$" for each 1" of beading, even when stretched in a frame. Take all of these factors into consideration when choosing fabrics and patterns. (See Figure 19)

Underlining

If the fabric will not support the weight of the beads, you must underline it. Underlining entails placing a second fabric behind the fashion fabric for bead and stitching support. The two fabrics are treated as one layer when stitching on the beads. Be certain to use a sturdy fabric for underlining. For sheer fabrics like chiffon and organdy, use multiple layers of the fashion fabric or use one or more layers of polyester or nylon organdy. Nylon organdy is stronger, but difficult to find. For opaque fabrics, use sturdy cotton muslin which comes in a variety of weights. Because the fashion fabric and underlining are treated as one layer, you must clean them both before beading if you plan to clean the project in the future. Two different fabrics will shrink at different rates the first time they are cleaned.

Interfacing

Interface beaded garments whenever possible. Interfacing helps a heavy garment maintain its shape. Since many beaded fabrics cannot be ironed because the beads will discolor or melt, use sew-in interfacing. Even if the fabric can be ironed, threads holding beads in place move during wear and cause iron-on interfacing to let go.

Lining

Whether for fashion or home decor, always line your beadwork. Lining protects threads on the back from getting caught, pulled, or broken. A lining also reduces stress on the outer fabric.

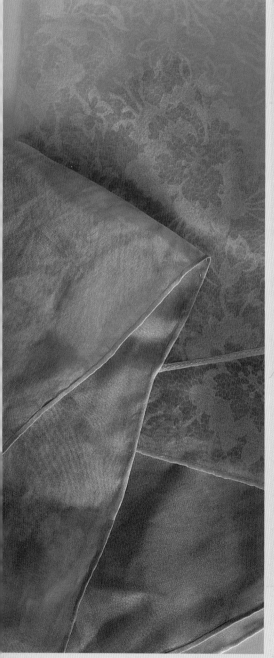

Figure 19

Knits

Knits can be beaded, but take special planning. Threads running from bead to bead on the back of the fabric reduce or eliminate stretch in the knit. If some areas are beaded and others not, one area may sag relative to the other. Spot-beading, knotting, and cutting the thread for every bead or tiny motif maintains stretch in a knit. Vertical beading, such as along the button band of a sweater, causes less distortion than horizontal beading because most knits stretch less in the vertical direction. For all-over beading of a knit, underline it with a woven fabric and treat the beaded knit as a woven fabric.

Lace

Lace yardage is beautiful when beaded; however, lace can be quite fragile. Bead in the structurally strongest part of the lace and underline the lace if necessary. Nylon or polyester organdy is used as a foundation for beaded lace appliqués. Nylon organdy under lace supports beads better because it is stronger and stiffer; however, a double layer of polyester organdy can be substituted. Polyester organdy comes in a wider range of colors including sparkly colors.

Ready-to-wear apparel

You can add beads to ready-to-wear apparel. If an underlining is necessary, place it only in the area behind the beads. If the garment is lined, try to hide threads running from one bead to the next between the fashion fabric and lining. If the fashion fabric needs more support, treat the lining as an underlining and stitch through both layers. Line again over the knots.

Beaded leaf design pillow
Embellished with seed and flat beads
Owned by Jill Grover

Supplies

Needles

Four types of needles are used for beading fabric: beading, sharps, milliners, and quilting betweens. Make your selection based on the length and stiffness of the needle. (See Figure 20)

Beading needles are long, thin, flexible needles with a very small eye. These come with either a twisted-wire shank or a solid shank. When beading on fabric, use needles with a solid shank. Beading needles are ideal for stringing beads on fringes, especially when you must pass the needle through each bead more than once. They are also used when a bead hole is too small for other types of needles.

Beading needles come in sizes from 10 (largest) to 16 (smallest). Use the largest size that will easily fit through the bead holes. A good rule of thumb is to use the same size beading needle as the size of the bead.

Sharps are common sewing needles used by seamstresses. They are shorter and stiffer than beading needles yet still have small eyes. Sharps are used when sewing only a few or individual beads onto fabric.

Sharps come in sizes 3 (largest) to 9 (smallest). Sizes 7 and 9 are the most useful for beadwork and will pass through all but the smallest seed beads. Sizes 10 and smaller are sometimes sold in bead stores as "short" beading needles.

Milliners needles are between beading needles and sharps in length. Use milliners needles to stitch several beads at one time onto fabric. They are also useful for stringing large bead fringes where the heavy thread required for such stringing will not fit through a smaller beading needle. Milliners needles come in the same sizes as sharps and can be found in most fabric and quilting shops.

Quilting betweens are short, sharp needles in small sizes. Their sizes range from 7 (largest) to 12 (smallest). Use them for sewing tiny individual beads onto fabric. They are also good when appliquéing completed motifs onto your outer fashion fabric.

Figure 20

26

Threads

Choose the thread according to your beads, fabric, and amount of use anticipated for the finished project. (See Figure 21) Select a color of thread to match either your beads or fabric, whichever one is less noticeable. Sewing thread is suitable for most beading projects. It is available in cotton, polyester, or a cotton-wrapped polyester core. Cotton has the advantage of not stretching, so beads stay tight against the fabric. But polyester thread is stronger. Cotton-wrapped polyester thread combines the best features of both. Double the thread for more strength and security.

Sewing thread comes in three weights: fine, all-purpose, and quilting thread. Select the weight of thread that will support your beads. Quilting thread is best for large faceted and fancy beads. Use fine thread only for very small seed beads. Choose a thread that fills the hole of the bead.

Multistrand nylon thread is best used for areas that will receive excessive use or where the thread needs to support heavy beads. Sizes range from F (largest), D, A, B, O, OO, to OOO (smallest). Size D is used for most purposes. Do not use nylon thread on lightweight or loosely woven fabrics because it will tear or distort the fabric. If nylon thread curls and knots as it comes from the spool, iron to straighten it.

Silk thread is traditionally used to couch metal threads.

Rayon thread can be used in the same applications as silk thread. Avoid using silk thread for general work. Like nylon thread, it can tear or distort the fabric.

Specialty threads are used when the look of the thread is important. Such threads must be strong enough to hold the beads in place, yet small enough to pass through the bead holes. Machine-embroidery threads are engineered to be strong enough to run through a sewing machine without breaking or stretching excessively. Synthetic-metal sewing thread is the most commonly used specialty thread. Gold is used with gold beads, silver with silver or clear beads. It comes in several other colors, as well, and may be flat or round. Use this type of thread to stitch beads that will be under spotlights. Thread peeking out of each end of the bead will give additional sparkle.

Figure 21

Glues

Whenever possible, avoid all types of glue in beadwork because they eventually decompose and they limit cleaning options. There is exception as in flat-backed stones, which do not have holes; sometimes the hole in a bead is not in the right place. In these cases, select the glue based on your purpose. (See Figure 22)

Use watch-glass cement to seal knots made in nylon thread. Nylon thread is slippery and knots eventually work loose. Washable fabric glue is used on the backs of completed appliqués to lock the fabric and threads holding the beads into place. Washable glues can be washed but not dry cleaned. Use fabric glue to adhere non-porous, flat-backed stones to fabric. (I use E6000 to stack or layer nonporous objects.)

Figure 23

Wax

Sometimes you will need to wax your thread before stitching beads. You can use either beeswax or synthetic thread conditioner. (See Figure 23) Beeswax smells good, but can stain white satin fabrics. Wax stiffens and straightens thread, but does not strengthen it.

Waxed thread twists and knots less than unwaxed thread because it is stiffer. You should wax general sewing thread. You can wax nylon thread if you like, but oftentimes it is not necessary. Do not wax specialty threads.

When sewing or stringing bugle beads, wax thread heavily. Bugle beads have sharp, unpolished edges and can cut through unwaxed thread.

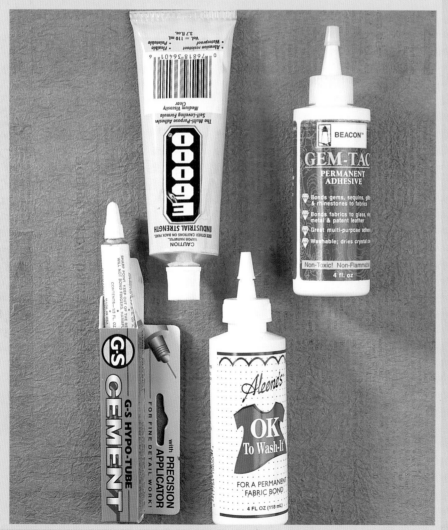

Figure 22

Beading patterns

Figure 24

The creative aspect of finding or developing a beading design can be one of the most difficult steps in beading. When looking for designs, examine the simple geometric shapes, quilting patterns, embroidery stitches, or construction details within the project such as collars, cuffs, edges, and hems.

The pattern or design within fabrics can be an inspiration for a beaded design. (See Figure 24) You can bead within fabric patterns, or use lines such as stripes as guidelines. When using an existing design, you can oftentimes bead without having to mark the placement of beads first.

Figure 25

Printed designs

Applying beads directly over a printed design is simplicity itself. Beads can be applied to all or part of a design. You will use this method more for casual wear than formal wear because formal fabrics are rarely printed. Printed fabrics are ideal for teaching beading to children. This printed design is used as the pattern for the placement of silver-lined seed beads and star nailheads. (See Figure 25)

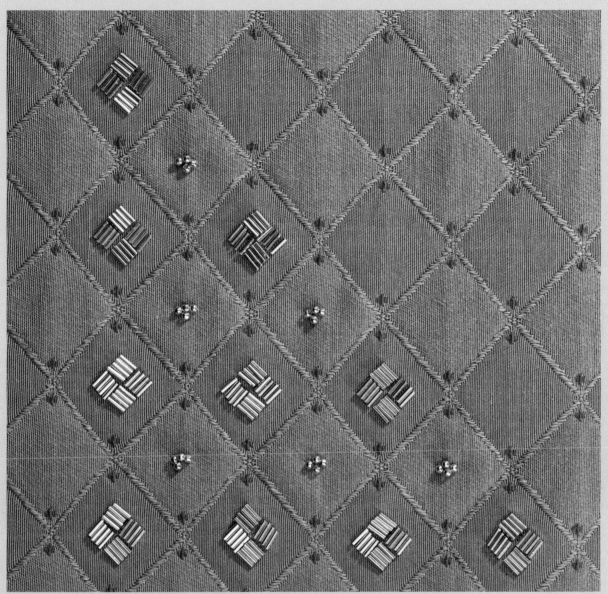

Figure 26

Pattern accents

Accenting designs within a fabric works well on many striped, tapestry, jacquard, and lace fabrics. Beading is done to highlight the design already in the fabric. Heavier tapestry and jacquard fabrics make great home furnishings such as pillows, and fashion accessories like vests and purses. The woven pattern in Figure 26 is accented with gold metal beads.

Figure 27

Sashiko

Japanese sashiko designs are composed of long lines of running stitches that intersect at various angles. The stitching lines may be straight or curved. Because the pattern uses only a running stitch, beads can be stitched into place quickly. Sashiko patterns are ideal for overall background beading.

Figure 28 is a sashiko-inspired beading design, using bugle beads on wool.

Figure 28

Quilting patterns

Quilting patterns use lines of individual stitches to hold multiple layers of fabric together and, at the same time, fill in background space. Each stitch can be easily embellished with a small bead. (See Figure 27)

Quilting patterns can also be beaded on a single layer of fabric simply as a design. Some quilting patterns are geometric patterns extended to an overall design.

More complex designs combine lines and curves to create flowing designs such as vermicelli, feathers, and wreaths. Beaders can find ready-to-use quilt patterns in the form of plastic stencils used for miniature quilts.

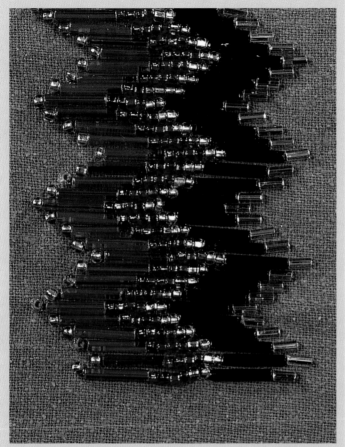

Figure 29

Florentine canvaswork patterns

Canvaswork patterns provide an inspiration for bead designs where solid coverage of the fabric is desired. Beads are attached to fabrics using these patterns, with long lazy stitches, then couched between adjoining colors to hold beads in place. (See Figure 29)

Bugle beads can be combined with seed beads to simulate a variety of canvaswork patterns. Varying the bead lengths, colors, and finishes produces the same feel as using different stitches. (See Figure 30)

Bugle-bead patterns are especially effective on lapels, collars, and vests.

Figure 30

Vermicelli

One of the most useful quilting patterns that is also used in beading is vermicelli. (See Figure 31) This continuous wandering line can be worked with either seed beads or bugle beads. The beads can touch each other or be spaced farther apart. Turns can be curved or angled. Because of vermicelli's wandering nature, some beads always catch the light no matter the angle viewed. Beading proceeds quickly, as the design is not carefully controlled, and when the design is completed, it looks as though there are more beads than there actually are.

Victorian pin cushion
*Black velvet embellished with
bead vermicelli & paper flowers*
Owned by Susan Ure

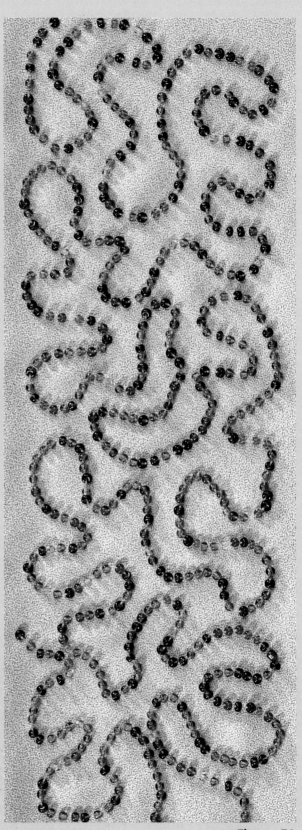

Figure 31

Victorian evening bag
Raw blue silk embellished
with seed beads
Owned by Susan Ure

Geometric designs

Simple geometric designs are ideal for both borders and allover designs. Traditional geometric shapes include Celtic knots, circles, diamonds, Greek keys, hexagons, squares, and triangles.

Repeating and stacking shapes allows a design to expand in any direction. (See Figure 32)

Doodle on graph paper to create your design, while keeping your lines straight and parallel.

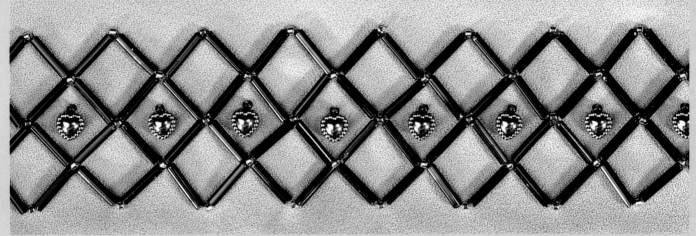

Figure 32

Figure 33

Embroidery stitches

Stitches and patterns from embroidery can be adapted to beading, such as traditional embroidery stitches, crazy-quilt stitches and motifs, silk-ribbon embroidery, Brazilian embroidery, and canvaswork.

Embroidery stitches can be beaded either by covering the exposed thread with beads or by using individual beads to substitute for stitches.

For examples of embroidery stitches such as the chain stitch and the herringbone stitch, (See Figure 33) fill the exposed thread with beads. Decorative motifs from crazy quilts and silk-ribbon embroidery often use French knots. Beaders use an individual bead to replace each French knot.

Short lengths of purl (metal) thread mimic bullion stitches, and strung beads wound around crossed needles form flowers in Brazilian embroidery.

Beaded purse
Embroidery-style beading

Beads can be used with traditional embroidery stitches and crazy-quilt stitches. (See Figure 34) Top to bottom: beaded chain stitch, crazy-quilt grape motif with beaded loops for leaves and individual beads replacing French knots for grapes, beaded crazy-quilt fan stitch, silk ribbon ladybugs with beads substituting for French knots, beaded herringbone stitch using seed beads and bugle beads.

Figure 34

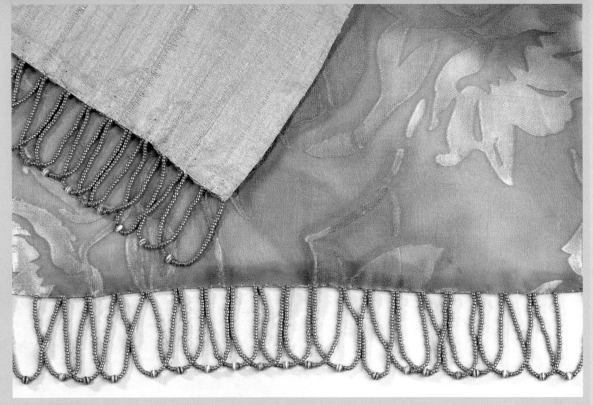

Figure 35

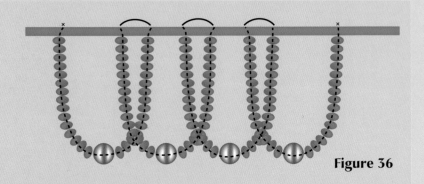

Figure 36

Construction details

Beading designs also can be inspired by construction details. As in the shawl above, a seam, a hem, the edge of a collar, cuff, or pillow, becomes a design feature instead of a necessary evil when embellished by a simple bead design. The shawl hem in Figure 35 is accented by beads that also serve as added weight to keep the shawl in place when wearing.

Shadow-beading (beading a short distance from and along the length of a seam or edge), narrow trims, fringes, and tassels are all popular ways to add beads. Beads in general, and fringes and tassels in particular, add weight to a piece and can improve the way a fabric drapes. Figure 36 illustrates a closeup view of the beading pattern used to fringe the shawl.

Pattern preparation

Once you have a design in mind, make a pattern. The first step is to draw the pattern on paper. If you plan to use the pattern extensively, you may want to make a more durable plastic stencil from the paper pattern.

Use whatever method you need to get the pattern on a sheet of paper—freehand sketching, drawing on graph paper, templates, or photocopy. You need not be an artist, you just need to indicate the placement of beads with a dot, line, or outline. You can use any type of paper you like; tissue paper, tracing paper, photocopy paper, graph paper, or newsprint are all acceptable.

Usually, you will start by making a test swatch of various parts of your design. Then by tracing, rotating, resizing, flipping, cutting, and pasting on your paper, you assemble a unified design. (See Figure 37) A light-table and a photocopy machine are great helps in making patterns. With a light-table, you can trace, flip, and rotate pieces. With a photocopy machine, you can resize and make multiple copies for repeats as done on the beading pattern to the right. Bead your design and repeat as desired. (See Figure 38)

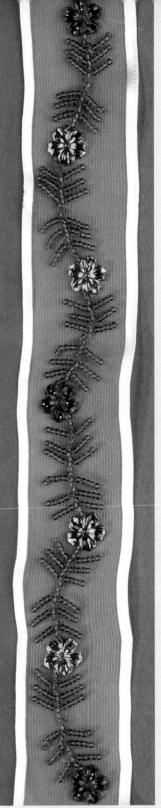

Figure 38

Figure 37

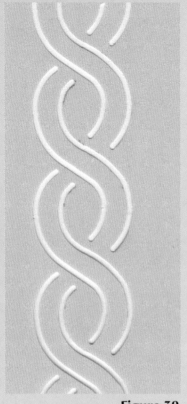

Figure 39

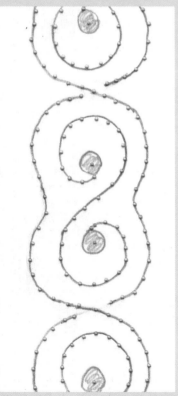

Stencil preparation

You can either make your own or purchase a commercial stencil. Commercial stencils for miniature quilts are ideal. (See Figure 39) It is worth your time to make a stencil from a paper pattern in two cases:

• when you use the pattern many times;

• when you need mirror images.

If you only intend to use a stencil a few times, you can make the stencil directly from the paper pattern. (See Figure 40)

To make a hand-pricked paper stencil:

1. Place the paper pattern on cardboard or Styrofoam® board.

2. Use a stiletto or large chenille needle to pierce holes along the pattern lines every ⅛"–¼". This is called pricking. Pierce holes closer together around curves and farther apart along straight lines.

Note: If you need mirror-image stencils, you can pierce two sheets of paper at one time, then turn one over for a reverse.

For a stencil that will be used repeatedly or that you will need to clean, use template plastic. You can find template plastic in most fabric and quilting stores.

To make a plastic stencil:

1. Tape the paper pattern to the back of the plastic template.

2. Place the plastic and pattern on a piece of scrap wood.

3. Drill small holes in the plastic along the pattern lines. An #80 wire drill bit works fine.

Figure 40

Pattern transferring

There are several methods to transfer a beading pattern onto fabric. Each method generally works best with certain types of fabrics. Do not be afraid to modify these methods to work for you.

Test the method on scrap material before trying it on your final fabric. You will usually transfer the beading pattern onto the fabric before lacing the fabric in the frame. Most marking methods leave a permanent mark on the fabric, so be certain to mark on the fabric only where the mark will be covered with beads.

Figure 41

Figure 42

Direct-paper transfer

The direct-paper method is good for sheer fabrics and for precise geometric designs. The paper pattern is attached to either the front or back of the fabric, using straight pins or basting stitches. (See Figure 42)

For sheer fabrics, copy the pattern onto tissue paper, attach it behind the fabric, and mount into the frame as one. Do not use cotton-rag paper; it will not tear away even when wet.

For opaque fabrics, attach the paper to the front of the fabric after it is mounted in the frame.

When beading, stitch through both the fabric and the paper. After beading is complete, tear away the paper. (See Figure 41) If the paper does not tear away easily, wet the paper. Use just enough water to dampen the paper. Do not allow the water to puddle on the fabric. Let the fabric dry thoroughly in the frame before removing the fabric. Beware, some copy and printer inks are water soluble and may run onto your fabric if you use too much water.

Figure 43

Ink on fabric method

The ink method is used for knitted, napped, woven, and fuzzy yarn fabrics. Mark the beading pattern on the fabric before mounting in a frame. Select a marker appropriate for the project:

Air-soluble markers are for beading projects you plan to finish that day.

Gel pens or permanent markers are for solidly beaded areas where the marking lines will be covered. Use on bumpy or firmly woven fabrics. (See Figure 43)

Pencils are used for firmly woven fabrics. A #2 lead pencil or quilt-marking pencil is recommended.

Water-soluble markers are for fabrics that can be washed. Remove marks by dabbing with a damp cloth while project is still in frame. Good for soft or loosely woven fabrics including knits.

Carbon transfer

The carbon-transfer method is good for large intricate designs on smooth, woven fabrics. You will mark the fabric before you mount it in a frame. Transfer the pattern from paper onto your fabric, using dressmaker's carbon, or transfer paper.

To create a carbon pattern:

1. Place a sandwich of fabric, carbon paper, and paper pattern on a hard surface. Make certain the right side is on the fabric.

2. With a hard-tipped object such as a stylus, trace over the pattern.

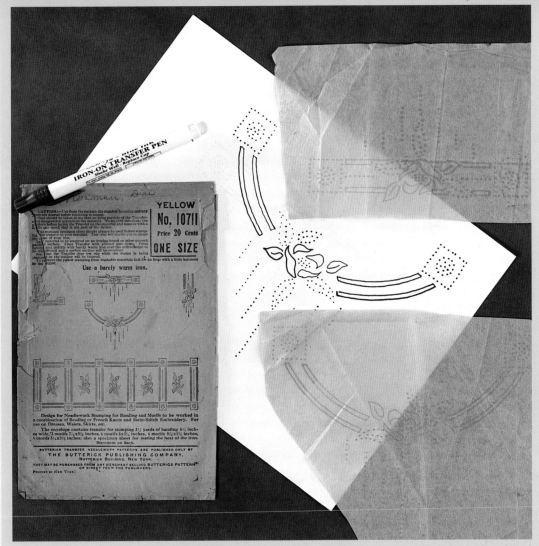

The above light brown, aged papers are cuff and neckline bead and embroidery iron-on transfers produced by the Butterick® Publishing Company, circa 1930. The reproductions of the transfers were made with iron-on transfer pens.

Iron-on transfer

Iron-on transfers can be used with any fabric that can be ironed at a moderate temperature. You can use commercial iron-on transfers or you can create your own. Follow the manufacturer's directions for application.

To create your own iron-on transfer:

1. Retrace lines with an iron-on transfer pen or pencil.

2. To make a mirror image of your paper pattern, photocopy it onto clear film, then reverse the film, or trace over the pattern placed upside down. A light-table or a sunny window works well.

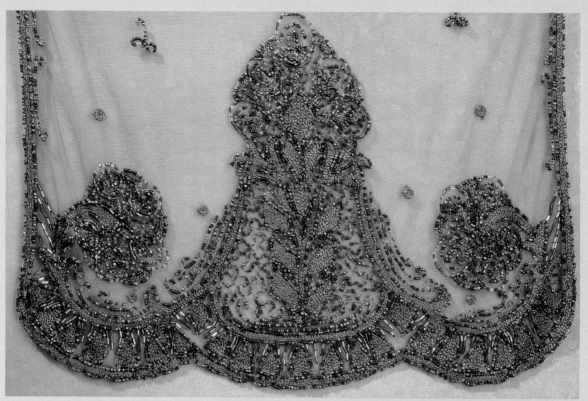

Antique sheer evening stole
Embellished with beads and embroidery
Owned by Susan Ure

Prick-and-pounce method

Prick-and-pounce is a good marking method to use when you have many repeats of the same pattern to mark. (See Figure 44 on page 45) It is the traditional method used to mark embroidery patterns at Lesage et Cie, the premier haute couture embroidery house in Paris. Marking should be done using a stencil, *after the fabric is mounted in the frame* as the pounce is delicate, smearing or fading into the fabric with the slightest jarring.

Any weight of paper or a lightweight plastic can be used for the stencil. You will smear chalk on your fabric if you try to flip a used paper stencil for the mirror image. To make a mirror image using a paper stencil, make two separate stencils; prick them simultaneously and flip one for reverse image. Make large margins on your templates or cover the fabric around the area you are marking to keep extraneous chalk off your fabric.

Notes: You can get powdered chalk in a variety of colors (black, red, blue) in a hardware store.

Always assume that pounce chalk will leave a permanent mark. Work carefully. The powder can be easily blown onto clean fabric or be smeared until set. You cannot clean chalk off of a paper stencil once it's been used.

To use the prick-and-pounce method:

1. Make a pounce "pad" by placing a few tablespoons of powdered chalk in the toe of a heavy athletic sock.

2. Tie the sock closed just above the chalk.

3. Place your stencil on top of the fabric with a solid support beneath. With plastic stencils, you can wash off any chalk, then flip the stencil over to create a mirror image.

4. Pounce the pad on top of the stencil by rubbing in a circular motion.

5. Set the chalk with two or three light coats of hair spray, holding the can at least 12" above the fabric. (See Figure 44)

Figure 44

Framing

Figure 45

Fabric preparation before framing

Fabric that will be mounted in a frame must be cut to fit into the frame and have its edges reinforced. (See Figure 45)

To fit fabric to an embroidery frame:

1. Determine where each pattern piece will lie on the fabric. Keep the width of the fabric to 28" or less so that it will fit in your frame.

2. Leave a margin of at least 4" around each pattern piece.

3. Cut or tear the fabric along the grain lines. This means that the cut line runs along a single weft or warp thread for the entire length or width of the fabric.

4. Reinforce all fabric edges. A strong edge is needed for attaching the fabric to the frame. Use either a narrow hem or reinforce edges with fray preventative for fine fabrics; or apply twill tape, using a wide zigzag stitch, for heavy fabrics.

Notes: Do not use bias tape, because it will stretch and not provide a sturdy edge. A woven-selvage edge need not be reinforced.

Outline pattern pieces

Outline the pattern pieces before you mount the fabric in the embroidery frame.

To outline a pattern piece:

1. Baste around the sewing lines of each pattern piece, using a contrasting color of thread.

2. Stitch so that 1"–3" of thread is exposed on top, followed by ¼"–½" of thread underneath.

3. Leave a 3"–4" tail and break thread at the end of each seam. Thread tails at ends of stitching lines make the thread easy to grab and pull out later. Be certain to outline the sewing line, not the cutting line. You want to know where to bead, not where to cut right now. Leave at least a 4" margin around each piece. This allows room for lacing the fabric onto the frame, seam allowances, and "shrinkage" of the fabric when it is beaded.

4. Baste center, front and back, darts, and other important features. You will re-mark the sewing and cutting lines after beading on the frame is completed to compensate for fabric "shrinkage." (See Figure 46) This half-scale bodice is basted to show the technique.

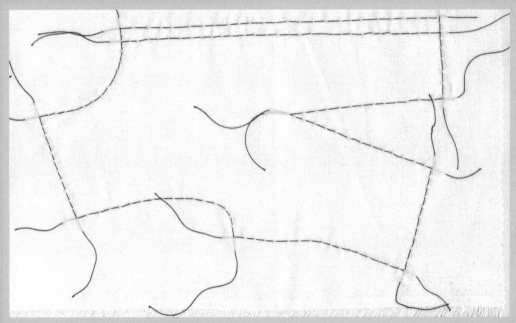

Figure 46

Embroidery hoops

Beading causes fabric to pucker or "shrink." Very small items or items with widely spaced beads can be embroidered without a frame. Small, widely spaced motifs, beaded edges and fringes, and simple neck, hem, and cuff trims on ready-to-wear apparel are examples of this type of item. Simply knot and cut the thread instead of running it across a distance to reduce shrinkage. Be certain you are not pulling the thread tightly enough to pucker the fabric.

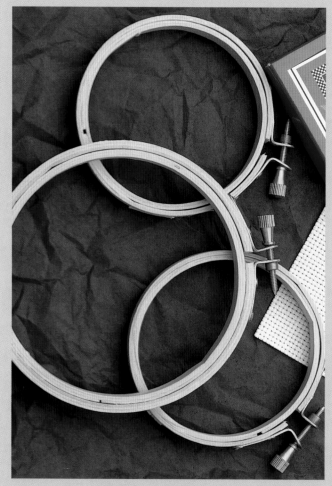

Figure 47

If you are stitching a small motif, use an embroidery hoop to keep your fabric flat. (See Figure 47) An embroidery hoop can be used for small pieces that fit entirely within the hoop.

The fabric must be placed on the grain and be drum tight in the hoop. Wrap both halves of the hoop with cotton-twill tape to grip the fabric better. You cannot reposition a hoop over completed beadwork because you cannot tighten the hoop sufficiently if beads lie between the layers of the hoop; and the hoop severely wrinkles fabrics that cannot be ironed.

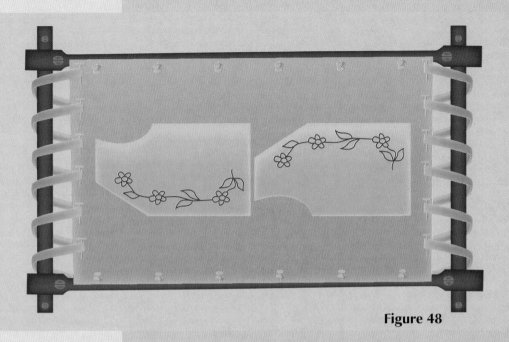

Figure 48

Beading frames

For large beading projects, use an embroidery "frame" that tensions your fabric both vertically and horizontally. Most fabrics cannot be ironed after beading and a frame helps keep the fabric wrinkle-free. You can rig up a frame with both vertical and horizontal tensioning from fixed–length stretcher bars and some scroll frames. (See Figure 48)

A slate frame consists of two pairs of stretcher bars. The length of the side bars is limited to 28" because you should be able to reach the center of the fabric from the top and bottom. The top and bottom bars can be any length. The length you choose depends on the size of your project or the amount of room you have to set up a frame.

With the edges of your fabric reinforced, the pattern pieces outlined, and the beading pattern marked, you are ready to mount and lace the fabric to the frame. You can use either strong thread, if the edges can withstand the strain, or twill tape.

The fabric is attached to the top and bottom bars by stitching it to the webbing attached to the bars or by stapling or thumbtacking the fabric directly to the bars. The fabric is then laced with strong thread or twill-taped to the side bars.

The slate frame is always used in a horizontal position. It is never tilted. You will need both hands free to work, so place the frame between two chair backs, tables, or commercial trestle legs. The frame should be positioned just above your bent elbow for a comfortable working height.

Lace fabric to frame

There are a number of different ways to lace your project in a frame. Choose the materials most appropriate for your project.

To mount to fabric:

1. Tack each end securely and evenly to the webbing on one of the horizontal bars.

2. If the fabric is longer than the vertical bars, roll the fabric onto one of the horizontal bars until the amount of fabric showing fits within vertical bars.

3. Mount the vertical bars in the slots or holes of the horizontal bars so the fabric is taut. The grainlines should be parallel to the bars; if not, straighten them.

4. Lace the vertical fabric edges to the vertical bars of the frame, keeping the grainlines parallel.

To lace with twill:

1. Using straight pins or safety pins, secure the twill tape close to one vertical edge of the fabric. (See Figure 49)

2. Pass the tape under then over the vertical bar. Move along the fabric edge about 1", fold the tape back, then pin the tape near the fold onto the fabric.

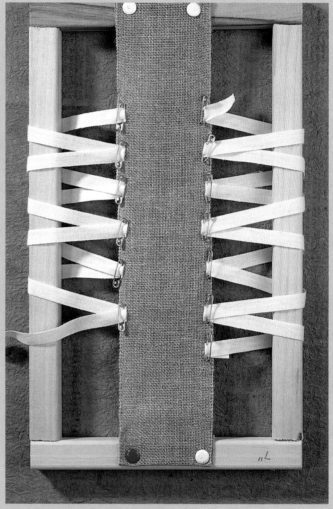

Figure 49

3. Repeat passing and pinning along the edge of the fabric, keeping an even tension on the fabric. Repeat for the other side.

Note: Repin the twill tape if necessary to keep an even tension on the fabric while beading.

50

To lace with thread:

1. Thread the needle with #10 cotton crochet thread in a length long enough to lace the entire side with one length of thread. Tie the thread to the vertical bar. Bring the needle from the back of the bar and up through the fabric. (See Figure 50)

2. Taking a 1" stitch along the vertical edge, go back down through the fabric. Pass the thread under then over the vertical bar. Repeat at 1" intervals for the length of the fabric.

3. Tie the remaining end of thread around the vertical bar, using a knot that can be easily removed. Repeat for the other side.

Note: Periodically untie and adjust the thread to keep an even tension on your fabric while beading.

Frame tips:

The following suggestions will make beading with a frame easier for you:

• If you have a limited amount of fashion fabric, stitch it onto a piece of muslin, then cut the muslin away from under the fashion fabric. Mount the larger piece of muslin onto the frame.

• When rolling completed beadwork onto one bar of a frame to expose an unbeaded area, pad the beaded area with machine-quilted fabric to protect the beadwork.

• Bead to within ½" of each seam. This allows room to machine-stitch the seams together (you cannot sew over beads). Complete the beading pattern over the seams after the seams are sewn, but before lining.

• When beading is complete, remove the work from the frame. Check the seam lines on each piece. They will probably not line up exactly with the thread basting due to "shrinkage" from the beading. Re-mark stitching and/or cutting lines for each piece. Remove the basting.

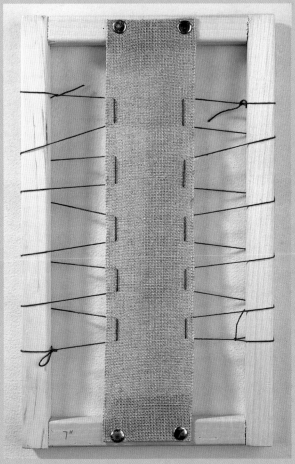

Figure 50

Stitching with beads

Handling beads

It may seem like a huge task to get all of those little beads where you want them. However, with a little practice and a few tips, you can handle beads quickly and efficiently.

Pour a few beads into a lightweight shallow container. You need to get each bead onto your needle and it's easiest to dig a bead out of a shallow container. Use a plastic lid from a food container, a tray with multiple divisions, or a plastic paint palette tray. Containers with white bottoms work best for dark beads, and vice versa. (See Figures 51 & 52 on page 53)

If you just turn a bag or tube of beads upside down and dump or just cut a string in a hank of beads, beads bounce all over. You need to control the beads.

For plastic bags, form a "V" in one side of the bag and pinch the rest of the opening closed. Touch the V to the bottom of a container and allow only a small stream of beads to flow out. If static electricity causes the beads to stick to the bag, blow into the bag. The moisture from your breath will remove the static.

For tubes, put your thumb over the opening and turn the tube upside down. Touch the tube to the bottom of a container and move your thumb slightly to allow a few beads to flow out.

For hanks, remove one strand of beads by gently pulling on both ends at the same time. Do not untie the knot holding the strands together. If the strand will not come free, clip the thread close to the knot. Lay the strand in a container. Pick up one end of the thread so the end is about 1" out of the container. Place two fingers of the other hand on the top bead. Without moving the fingers on the top bead, gently pull up on the thread to remove it.

Figure 51

Stringing beads

Pick up a bead from a container by pressing the needle tip on the bead hole. The bead will pop onto the needle. Use your finger to hold the bead on the shaft of the needle.

If stringing beads onto a thread, as for a fringe, pop the beads onto the needle one at a time, holding the last bead on the needle with your finger.

If you need a number of beads on a thread, start with a pile of beads and push the needle through the middle of the pile. With each pass, a few beads will be threaded onto the needle.

If stringing a lot of beads, a bead spinner speeds up the process. With a bead spinner, hold the needle stationary in a spinning bowl of beads and the beads magically jump onto the needle.

Figure 52

Threading your needle

The eyes on beading needles are so small, you will need to learn to thread needles by hand.

1. Cut the end of the thread cleanly with sharp embroidery scissors. Wet the end of the thread in your mouth and flatten the end between your front teeth or use your fingernails.

2. Pinch the flattened end between your thumb and index finger. Let about ¹⁄₁₆" thread peek out between your fingers. Align thread with the elongated hole in the eye. Push the eye of the needle onto the end of the thread. At the same time, slowly spread the tips of your thumb and index finger, forcing the thread through the eye. Pinch end and pull thread through needle. The eye is wider in the middle than at the ends, so position the thread in the center as you are pulling it through.

Tying knots

After threading the needle, double the thread and make a rolled knot in the end. If a knot will leave a bump that will show on the front of the fabric, take two or three stitches through the fabric on top of one another in a place that will be covered with beads.

Some slippery threads will not hold a knot. Seal both the beginning and ending knots in these threads with a small drop of watch glass glue. Tie extra knots before and after large individual beads and periodically in running and couching stitches.

Mother's Queen-for-a-Day crown
Crescent board, sheer silk,
gold cording, and beads
Owned by Susan Ure

Types of stitches

Having designed the project and gathered the supplies, you are ready to stitch beads. There are many different stitches that can be used to attach beads and embellishments to fabric. This section provides a repertoire of stitches to choose from and introduces you to most of the stitches and techniques you will use to secure beads and embellishments to fabric.

Figure 53

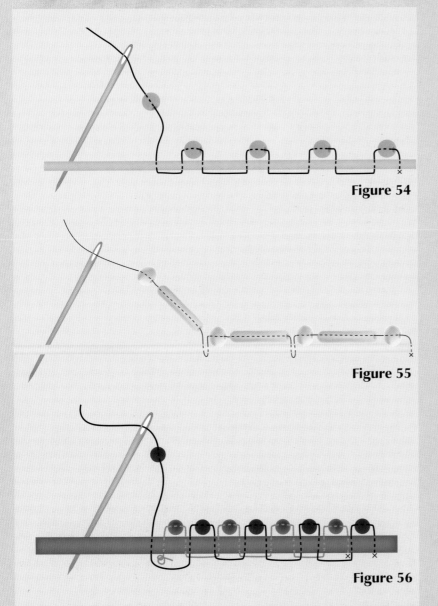

Figure 54

Figure 55

Figure 56

Running stitch

A running stitch is the fastest way to sew beads onto fabric in either a straight or curved line. It is made by bringing the needle up through the fabric, through a bead, and then down through the fabric. The process is repeated, spacing the beads a short distance apart. (See Figure 54)

The running stitch can be modified for special applications. One use is to stitch multiple beads into place with each stitch. For example, this application is often used when adding a seed bead to the end of a bugle bead. (See Figures 53 & 55) This helps prevent the bugle bead from cutting through the thread.

Double running stitch

A running stitch cannot be used to sew beads right next to each other unless two passes of running stitch are made which is then called a double running stitch. (See Figure 56)

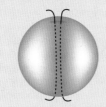

Figure 57

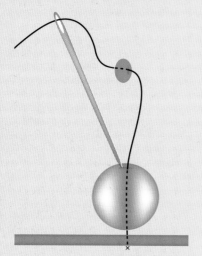

Figure 58a

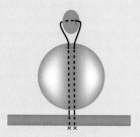

Figure 58b

Figure 59

Stitching single beads

Most of the time you will attach a bead to fabric, using a single stitch. (See Figure 57) However, sometimes, especially with large beads, you may want to stabilize the bead, disguise the stitching thread, or hide the hole by using other techniques. Different methods for sewing individual beads are shown in Figure 59. From left to right the beads are stitched with two stitches, metallic thread, beaded thread, purl over thread, stop bead.

Large beads sewn onto the fabric with a single stitch often slip and slide about. You can stabilize the bead by stitching through the hole twice, spacing the stitches slightly farther apart than the width of the hole.

When sewing small beads, the sewing thread is barely visible, but with larger beads, the thread is noticeable if other beads are not stitched right next to it. The thread can be disguised or blended into the beadwork in a number of ways. One way is to stitch the bead in place with metallic thread. This adds sparkle to garments under a spotlight.

Another way to cover thread is to bead over the thread, using seed beads. (See Figures 58a & b) The seed beads and purl covering the thread run completely through the hole of the large bead. Most times, the seed beads and purl will just cover the thread showing between the fabric and the hole of the large bead.

Backstitch

Like the running stitch, the backstitch is used to sew single beads in a straight or curved line. Figure 60 shows nested squares stitched in various seed beads and bugle beads, all with backstitch.

The backstitch is more secure and stable than the running stitch because it passes the thread under the fabric twice for each stitch. (See Figure 61)

The backstitch is made by bringing the needle up through the fabric at the far end of the bead placement, stringing on the bead, then down through the fabric again at the near end of bead placement, passing underneath the fabric, and finally coming back up at the far end of the next bead placement.

The nested squares to the right are stitched in various seed beads and bugle beads, all with backstitches.

Figure 60

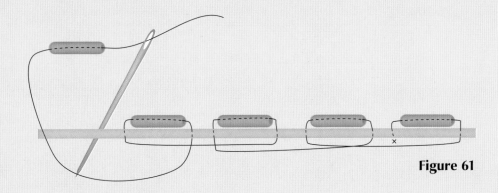

Figure 61

Figure 62

Lazy stitch

The lazy stitch is used to attach several beads with a single stitch. Figure 62 is beaded leaf trim stitched on nylon organdy, using the leaf pattern in Figure 63. Lazy stitches secure the beads (See Figure 64) while backstitches secure the sequins. The basic lazy stitch is stitched like a running stitch with several beads strung on each stitch. Usually the beads are placed so they touch both horizontally and vertically, giving a pavé look. The beads stack together tightly with no gaps between them. The stitch is not very secure, having little or no thread on the back of the fabric to support the beads. For this reason, it is frequently used on knits to help maintain the flexibility of the fabric.

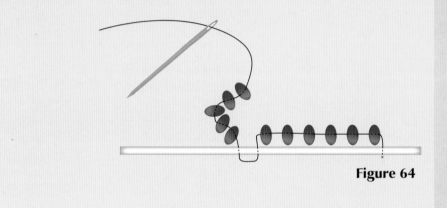

Figure 64

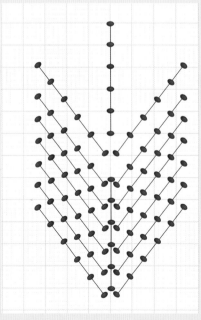

Figure 63

Lazy satin stitch

There are several variations of the lazy stitch. Figure 65 is an expanded lazy "satin" stitch to show stitch clearly. Beads would normally touch both horizontally and vertically.

The lazy satin stitch conserves thread by work–ing back and forth in parallel or nearly parallel rows, taking a stitch only large enough to position the thread at the beginning of the closest end of the next row.

Figure 66 uses a lazy satin stitch worked around a rattail cord placed in the fold of the hem.

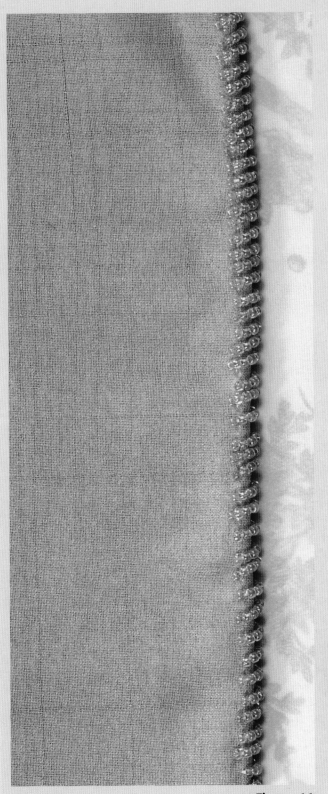

Figure 66

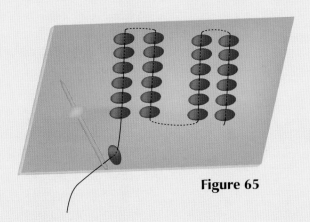

Figure 65

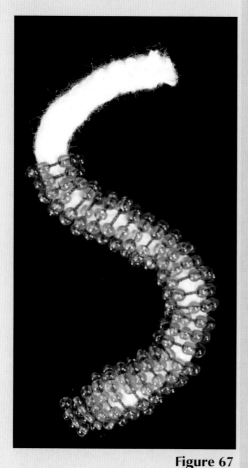

Figure 67

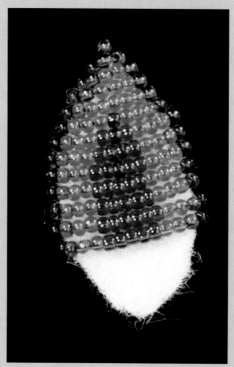

Figure 68

Padded lazy satin stitch

Padding a lazy satin stitch increases relief and helps keep beads from sinking into fabric. On velvet it is used to raise beads out of the nap. Felt or upholstery cord is traditionally used for padding. Figure 67 is beaded over cord while Figure 68 is beaded over felt. Use padding that matches the color of your fabric.

When using cord, taper the core of the cord for ½"–1", then stitch down firmly. (See Figure 69)

Felt can be cut to shape and multiple layers used for more relief. When using multiple layers, cut each layer slightly smaller than the preceding one. Arrange them with the smallest layer next to the fabric and the largest one on top. This will give the smoothest finish.

The padded lazy satin stitch is stitched like a backstitch with several beads strung on each stitch. (See Figure 70) The stitch is more stable than a traditional lazy stitch because there is a length of thread across the back of the fabric for each stitch. (See Figure 71)

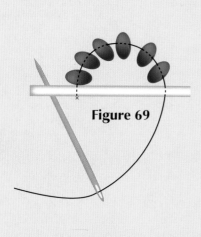

Figure 69

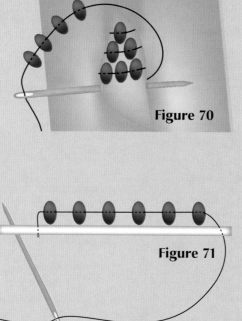

Figure 70

Figure 71

Beaded purse
Owned by Susan Ure

Raised lazy stitch

A raised lazy stitch is formed when the stitch length is shorter than the combined length of the beads strung on the stitch. (See Figure 69 on page 60) The short thread pushes the beads out from the fabric. It can be stitched with either a lazy stitch or a lazy satin stitch. The lazy stitch version is the one most often used in Native American beading. The lazy satin stitch version is the one used for making beaded ropes and cables.

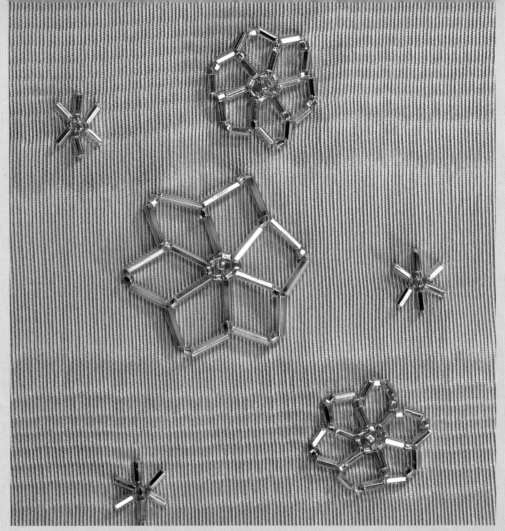

Figure 72

Couching stitch

Couching is used to attach beads or embellishments that are already strung together on a separate string onto fabric. (See Figure 72) Prestrung beads and embellishments that need to be "couched" onto a fabric come from a variety of sources. Some beads, including pearls, sequins, and rhinestones can be purchased prestrung. Watch the quality of prestrung beads. Often they are cheap plastic molded onto the string.

Sometimes, you will make your own strung trims as in the stars in Figure 73, because it is faster to string the beads and couch them in place than to sew each bead in place one at a time. Other times, you will want to use long lines of lazy stitch so that the beads stack together tightly but the lines become so long they flop about. A few couching stitches can hold these beads in place. (See Figure 74 on page 63)

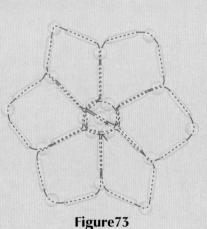

Figure 73

62

To work the couching stitch (See Figure 75):

1. Position the prestrung beads on the fabric.

2. Bring needle up through fabric, directly under the thread holding the strung beads.

3. Pass the needle over the thread holding the beads. Go back down through the same hole where you came up.

4. Tighten the couching thread so it sits between the beads and on top of the thread holding the beads, but does not pull the thread holding the beads down to the fabric. For heavy beads and bead threads forming tight curves, couch between every bead. On straight lines, couch every few beads as needed to hold the thread in place.

Notes: You may find it easier to couch using two needles and thread. The first needle and thread strings the beads and the second does the couching.

The two-needle technique works well for couching long lazy stitches and long lines of beading where it is easier to manage the beads if you only string a few at a time.

Black velvet hat
Embellished with beads
Owned by Susan Ure

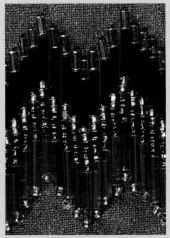

Figure 74

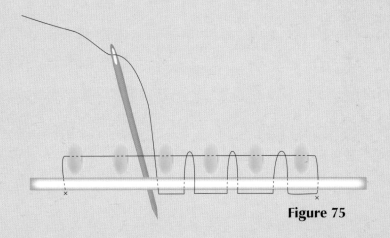

Figure 75

Making dangles

Figure 76

Dangles combine stitching and stringing to produce beadwork that stands away from the fabric. (See Figure 76) Unattached at one end, dangles are free to move. Dangles become little fringes when worked on the edge of the fabric. Combinations of bead size, color, and shape produce an endless variety of dangles.

Dangles use one of two methods for attachment to the fabric: single point or two point. Single-point attachment creates a dangle that emanates from a single spot, focusing attention on that spot. Two-point attachment produces a dangle that moves the eye.

Strong thread is needed to support strung beads. Use a double strand of quilting thread whenever possible. For the smallest seed beads and some stringing that requires multiple passes through a bead you may need to use smaller thread.

Figure78

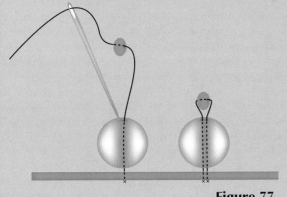

Figure 77

Stop bead

A large bead can be stitched with the hole perpendicular to the fabric, using a stop bead. Bring the needle up through the fabric, the large bead, and a seed bead, then back down through the bead and fabric. (See Figure 77)

Figure 78 is a commercial sample of a simple dangle composed of a drop and a seed stop bead used as the flower's stamen.

Figure 79

Single-point attachment

Single-point dangles are formed by having the thread pass through several beads and then pass back through the first bead and possibly others in the opposite direction. They are elaborate variations of the stop bead.

Individual dangles are placed with a single stitch. Multiple dangles are stitched with a running stitch. They can be used to add dimension and movement. The patterns for the dangles in Figure 79 are shown in Figure 80. The top two right dangles, though sewn in straight lines, create curled shapes when the stitch is pulled snugly. The bottom left is an ultrasuede cut-out flower with dangle stamens stitched in a group. The bottom right is an example of multiple dangles stitched in a line with a running stitch.

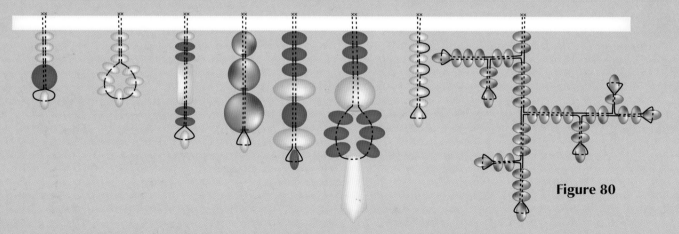

Figure 80

Two-point attachment

For a two-point attachment, thread leaves the fabric through one bead and enters the fabric through another bead. (See Figure 81) Multiple dangles can be stitched with either a running stitch or backstitch to form lines or groups of raised beadwork.

Multiple dangles stitched with a running stitch make informal lines or groups. (See right row of Figure 81 and Figure 83) The tops are separate and free to move, which can sometimes create an unkempt look. Dangles using a two-point attachment can be tied together or overlapped, using a backstitch to form denser, more cohesive lines and groups. (See left row of Figure 81 and Figure 82) In such a case, the dangles must move as a group, creating a more formal, restrained look.

Figure 81

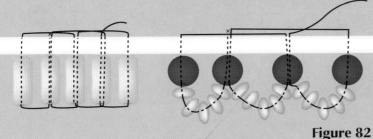

Figure 82

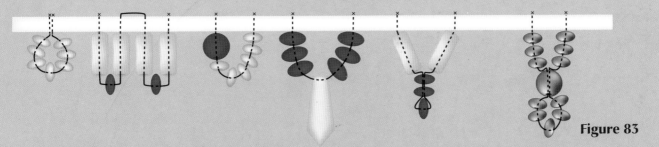

Figure 83

67

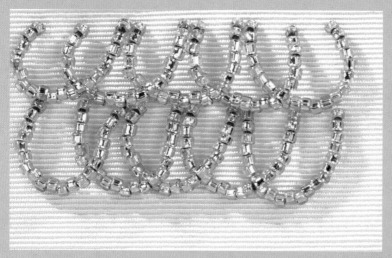

Figure 84

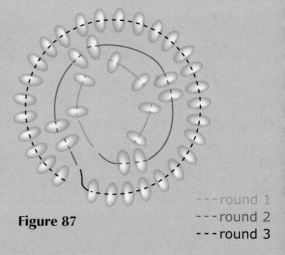

Figure 85

Figure 86

Figure 87

- - - round 1
- - - round 2
- - - round 3

The multiple dangle in Figures 84 and 86 is stitched with a backstitch. The golden flower in Figure 86 is formed from dangles stitched in a group. Each stitch contains an oval bead, three seed beads, and then an oval bead. Figure 87 details the formation of the flower's center.

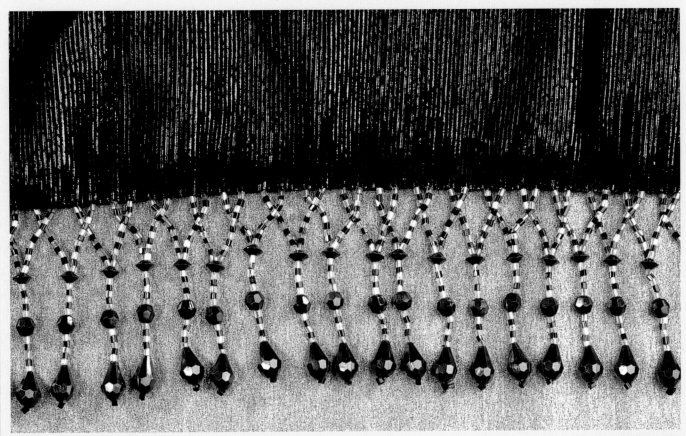

Figure 88

Making fringes

Long, individual dangles stitched next to each other make a fringe. Fringes can be made using either the single-point attachment or two-point attachment method.

The fringe on the shawl in Figure 88 was made with two-point attachment of individual dangles. (See Figure 89) The dangles were stitched on a header and inserted into the fabric seam.

Fringes are usually seen on the edge of a fabric but are sometimes used in the middle to divide a piece or cause the eye to travel.

Figure 89

Fringe headers

Fringe is heavy, therefore needs a lot of support. Strong fabrics or reinforced edges (stay) can have fringe stitched directly onto them. You can use the selvage retained on the edge of the fabric to act as a stay by turning it under in place of a hem. In other instances, it is better to stitch the fringe on a separate header and then attach the header to the fabric. The header functions as a stay and helps distribute the weight of the fringe evenly along the fabric edge.

Any strong tape, ribbon, or trim such as twill tape, satin ribbon, grosgrain ribbon, or decorative trim can be used for a header. (See Figure 90)

When stitching on woven headers, such as twill tape and ribbon, place the first stitch just above the selvage, which is the strongest part of the header.

A flat header-like twill tape or ribbon is stitched inside a seam or behind an edge or hem. Textured, decorative trims, such as rickrack, braid, and trim, are applied directly to the surface of the piece.

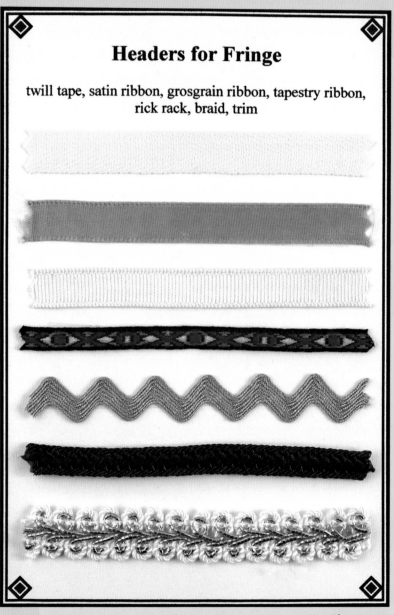

Headers for Fringe

twill tape, satin ribbon, grosgrain ribbon, tapestry ribbon, rick rack, braid, trim

Figure 90

70

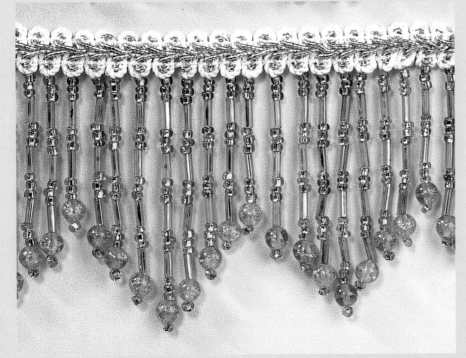

Figure 91

Fringes are stitched on headers, using single-point attachment. In Figure 91, yellow cracked-glass ball, silver-lined yellow seed beads, and bugle beads where combined. While in Figure 92, blue dagger, black twisted-bugle beads, silver-lined blue and matte black seed beads were strung together. Seed beads at either end of the bugle beads protect the thread from being cut by sharp-edged bugle beads.

Stitch the fringes with strong thread. Use quilting thread whenever possible. Wax the thread heavily when using bugle beads to prevent the sharp edges from cutting the thread.

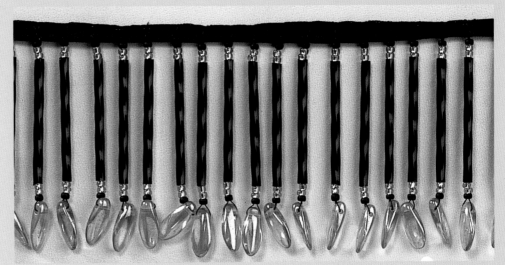

Figure 92

Woven Ribbons

weave/material (top to bottom): organdy, taffeta, satin, velvet, grosgrain, metallic, tapestry

Figure 93

Woven ribbons

Ribbons are manufactured with either a plain or a wired edge. Both are used in beadwork. Wires woven into the selvage are used to shape a ribbon. If you see a wired ribbon that you like but do not want the wire, just pull the wire out. (See Figure 93)

For additional support, take tiny stitches through the header, straight up from the dangle to the other selvage, along that selvage to the location for the next dangle, and then down to the first selvage, like an upside down U.

You may want to tie a knot after each dangle in the event a dangle breaks, you only lose a few beads.

Figure 94a

Figure 94b

Figure 95a

Figure 95b

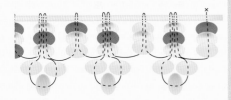

Figure 95c

Figure 96

Picot edges

A picot edge is a beaded fringe in which the ends that would be free in a dangle are tied together. (See Figure 96) The thread passes from picot to picot through the beads, unlike dangles where the thread passes from dangle to dangle through the fabric.

A small pick stitch is used to attach each picot to the fabric. To make a pick stitch, pass the needle from the front to the back through the fold or edge of the fabric, catching just a few threads of the fabric. (See Figures 94a & b) The stitch is perpendicular to the surface of the fabric.

Picots are used as a simple edging or as a foundation for nets. When used as edging, decorative beads may be incorporated. When used as a foundation for netting, beads are composed of plain seed beads, usually the same beads that are used elsewhere in the net.

Picots may be spaced to touch one another or may be spaced farther apart but the edging begins to lose its integrity if picots are spaced more than a bead width apart. Variations in the basic pattern are numerous. (See Figures 95a–c)

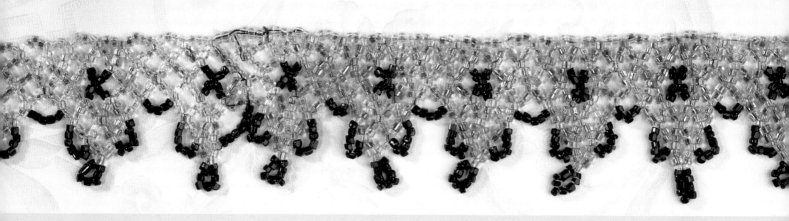

Figure 97

Making nets

Nets are fringes in which the dangles are attached to their neighbors to add stability. (See Figure 98) Nets have a more unified look than fringe and are more stable. Nets may be stitched directly onto the edge of fabric, onto a header, or onto a picot edge. Occasionally, a net is formed in the middle of fabric with all of the edges tacked to the fabric.

Nets use large amounts of beads and thread. Start with enough thread to make one complete row of net and tie the thread off in the fabric. This may incorporate as much as six yards of thread. To keep this amount of thread from tangling, wax it heavily. If you must add thread in the middle of a row, run the thread through several beads in another row and then knot the thread between beads and around the thread of the other row. Seal the knot with cement if you think it might not hold.

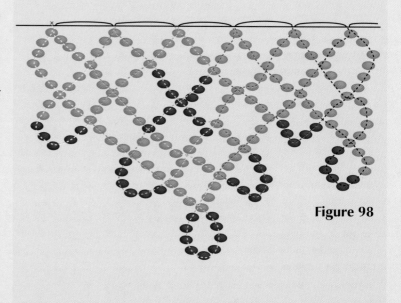

Figure 98

Many nets include dangles along the bottom edge. The dangles are strung as the net is formed. Most dangles on net use a variation of the single-point attachment but a two-point attachment is possible.

The elaborate 1930s vertical net in Figure 97 is made of silver-lined clear and black seed beads. The silver lining has oxidized to a gray. Although this net is unattached from fabric, it could be couched into place or made directly on the fabric.

Horizontal net

Horizontal net are formed by stringing beads in horizontal rows. The net in Figure 99 is directly attached to the fabric, using a two-point attachment for each dangle. The first row is attached to the fabric, header, or picot edge. Succeeding rows are attached to the last row of beads. Where rows meet, beads are used twice, once by each row. (See Figure 100)

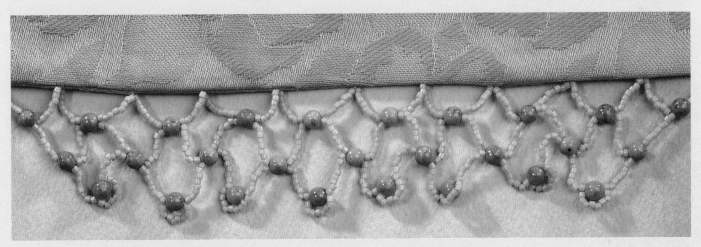

Figure 99

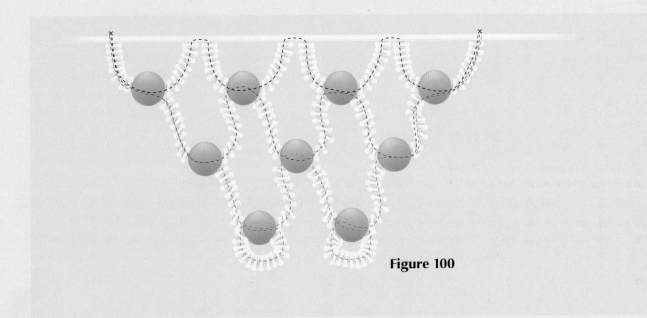

Figure 100

Figure 101

Looped net

Looped net, also known as brick stitch or Comanche stitch, is formed by stringing beads in horizontal rows. (See Figure 101) This looping method forms a solid net. It is on a picot row and uses a single-point attachment for dangle.

The first row is attached to the fabric or header, using a pick stitch. Succeeding rows are joined by passing the thread through a bead, looping it over the thread between beads in the previous row, and then passing the thread back through the same bead in the opposite direction. This looping method forms a solid net. Each row is offset from the previous row. (See Figure 102 on page 77)

Variations of looped net include a triangular looped net (See Figure 103) or a rectangular looped net (See Figure 104). Any variation can secure a dangle attachment as shown in Figure 105.

Figure 102

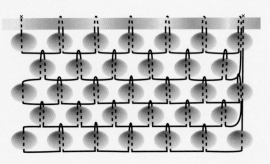

Figure 104

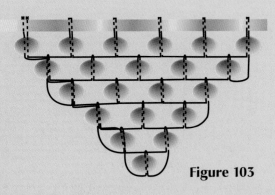

Figure 103

Figure 105

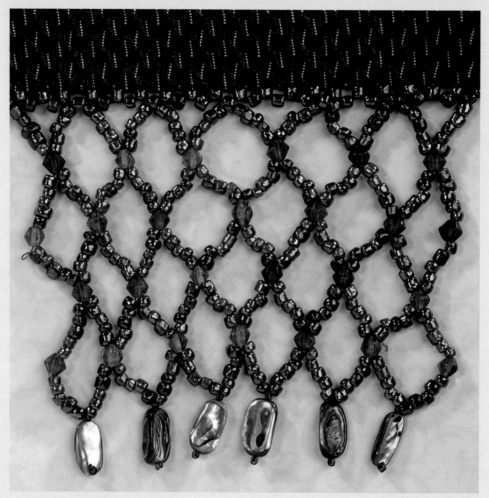

Figure 106

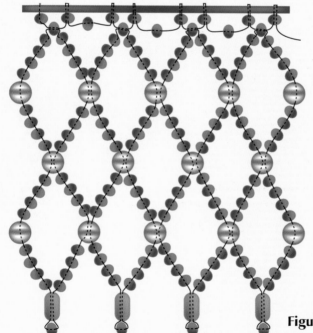

Vertical net

Vertical net is formed by stringing beads in vertical rows. Every other row is attached to the fabric, header, or picot edge. Where rows meet, beads are used twice, once by each row.

The vertical net in Figure 106 is on a picot row. This net uses a single-point attachment for dangle. (See Figure 107)

Figure 107

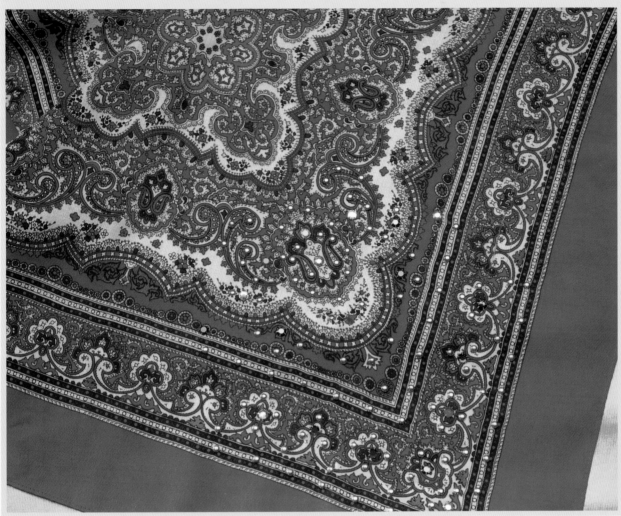

Figure 108

Embellishments used with beads

Embellishments are often combined with beads in a design. These include sequins, rhinestones, cabochons, shisha, nailheads, buttons, metal threads, braids, cords, and ribbons. From a design point, these related embellish-ments add texture, movement, and interest. From a mechanical point, they help reduce the weight of beadwork and the large size relative to most beads decreases the time needed to complete a project. (See Figure 108)

Sequins

The most common shape for a sequin is flat and round with a single hole in the middle. Some sequins have three-dimensional shaping produced by cupping (couvette) and crimping. Surface finishes may be shiny or matte. Sequins with hologram finishes reflect nearly as much light as faceted beads. Plastic is the most common material, metal less so. Natural material sequins such as straw, beetle wings (a trademark of the Thai royal family), or fish scales are used for special projects.

Sequins are available prestrung in several formats. They can be strung by themselves in a single row. Multiple rows may be strung on a firm thread or on elastic. Sequins may also be incorporated into a decorative braid or used to embellish lace trims.

Like beads, most sequins have a single hole that can be used to attach it to fabric, using many of the same stitches that are used for beads. Sequins can be individually spaced or overlapped.

Below the prestrung sequins in Figure 109 is a variety of shapes and finishes. Interesting shapes such as hologram finished, crimped circle, cupped star, and decorative S shapes are shown. Also illustrated are flat shapes such as a small star, hexagon with matte finish, decorative snowflake, four small shapes that are either crimped or cupped, flower with iris finish and paillette which is a type of sequin with the hole near an edge so the shape can hang freely.

The bottom row includes an imitation coin traditionally used on belly-dancing costumes, metal sequins, and a mother-of-pearl paillette.

Sequins

Sequins were originally flat metal circles with a single hole in the middle for attachment. Sequins are still relatively flat but can be cupped or crimped, come in a wide variety of shapes, are usually plastic and may have more than one hole for attachment. Paillette generally refers to a shape with the hole at one edge so it can hang free. Common sizes range from 3 mm to 12 mm although some range up to 30 mm.

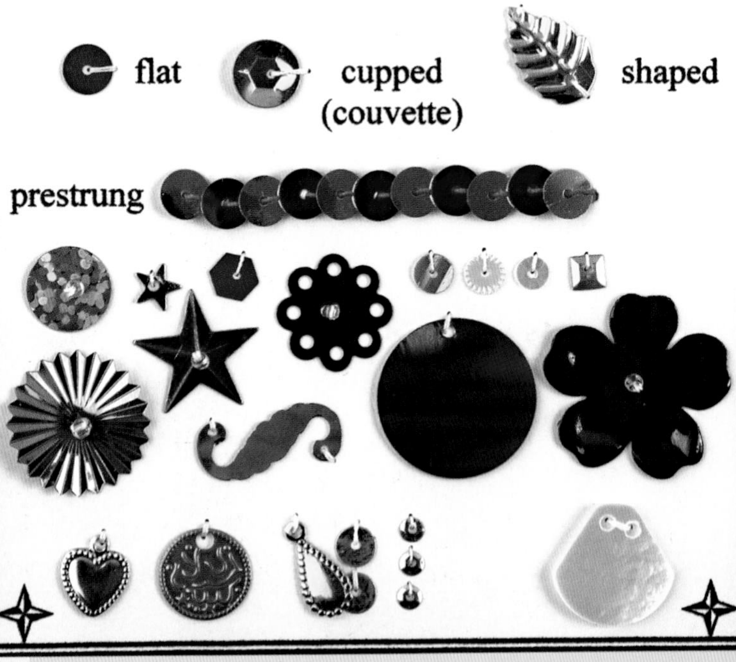

flat   cupped (couvette)   shaped

prestrung

Figure 109

When spaced as individual sequins a stop bead, running stitch, or backstitch can be used to hold each sequin in place. (See Figure 110) The stitching thread will be exposed so use a matching color, metallic, or cover with seed beads or purl. This is one time you might want to use a single thread for stitching.

Sequins can be overlapped using a running stitch or backstitch. The overlap can cover the stitching thread or the thread can be left exposed. If exposed and covered with seed beads or purl, it looks as if a solid line of beads or purl is stitched over the sequins.

When using a running stitch to secure overlapping sequins, the stitch does not follow a straight line.

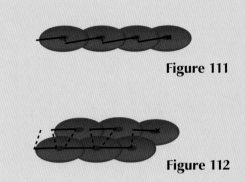

Figure 111

Figure 112

To stitch a single line: (See Figure 111)
1. Stitch up through the center hole of the first sequin and down along the edge in the desired direction.

2. Take a tiny stitch perpendicular to the direction you want to go and just at the edge of the sequin you just attached.

3. Slip the next sequin on the needle (which is the same as stitching up through the center hole of the first sequin) and repeat the process.

To stitch a double line: (See Figure 112)
1. Stitch up through the center hole of the first sequin and down along the edge in the direction you wish to go.

2. Move at a 45-degree angle down along the edge of the sequin and bring your needle to the top.

3. Thread on the next sequin and stitch along the edge of the sequin in the desired direction. This stitch will be parallel to and offset from the first stitch by the width of a sequin.

4. Move at a 45-degree angle up the edge of this sequin to where the first stitch ended, thread on the next sequin, and repeat.

Figure 110

Figure 113

Common stitches for sequins are shown in Figure 113. On the top row the individual sequins are stitched with stop beads, running stitch with matching blue and metallic red threads, star with exposed thread covered with beads, purple sequins with exposed thread covered with purl. The middle row shows overlapping sequins stitched with a running stitch in a single line and a double line. The sequins in the bottom row are backstitched so the thread is covered or backstitched so thread is exposed—exposed thread red metallic thread, blue seed beads, and gold purl.

When sewing individual sequins you may apply overlapping sequins with a backstitch. The threads may be covered as in Figure 114a on page 83, or exposed as in Figure 114b. Other options include: using a running stitch covering exposed threads with beads or purl (See Figure 114c) Using a running stitch covered with beads or purl. (See Figure 114d) Using a running stitch with exposed thread. (See Figure 114b) Using a stop bead to conceal the thread. (See Figure 114e)

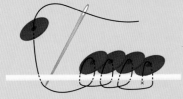

Figure 114a

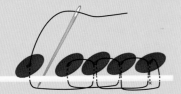

Figure 114b

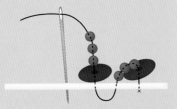

Figure 114c

Figure 114d

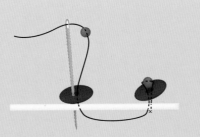

Figure 114e

Beaded scarf
*Design embellished
with sequins*

83

Figure 115

Figure 116

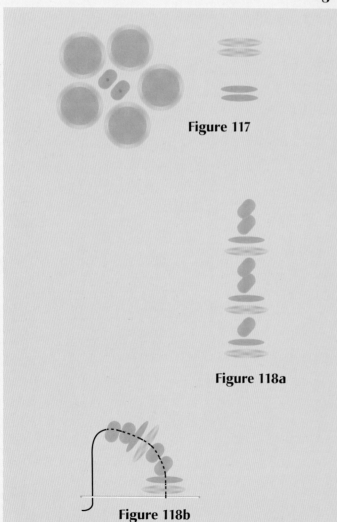

Figure 117

Figure 118a

Figure 118b

Sequins may be stacked to produce three dimensional motifs. Cupped sequins are usually used and stacked together, with the cups back to back, or sequins are spaced with beads to give height and separation. (See Figures 115 & 116)

To stitch Figure 115:
1. Stitch two back-to-back cupped sequins in five positions around a circle. Pull each stitch snug so that the unstitched edges of the sequins spread up.

2. Offset the second layer from the first to fill the gaps.

3. Stitch ten back-to-back sequins into the center with a single stitch. (See Figure 117)

To stitch Figure 116:
1. Arrange the beads in a stack in the following order: one flat sequin, one cupped sequin, two seed beads, one flat sequin, one cupped sequin, and two seed beads.

2. Stitch into each of six locations around a circle. The flat sequin is slightly larger than the cupped sequin. Use the stitch to pull the stack tight, producing a U-shaped stitch that bends the top two beads down toward the fabric.

3. Stitch the following stack of beads in the center: one flat sequin, one cupped sequin, and one seed bead. It will be held off of the fabric by the top two beads of each stack. (See Figures 118a & b)

Rhinestones & other flat-backed stones

Large faceted beads reflect a lot of light but they are heavy and bulge out from the fabric. When the weight of the beads or the depth of a design becomes a concern, flat-backed rhinestones, cabochons, mirrors (shisha), or nailheads might be a substitute. (See Figure 119) The flat backs on these embellishments reduce the weight by using "half" a bead. The flat back also provides more stability and the design profile is kept low.

Of all the embellishments used with beads, flat-backed stones have the greatest variety of attachment methods. These methods include sew-on, mount in metal rims, thread frames, and glue, fuse, and tape. You will not do very many beading projects before you have tried them all.

The most common type of flat-backed stones used in beading are rhinestones and cabochons. Cabochons are round or oval stones with a smooth rounded top. They are made from glass, acrylic, gemstones, and pearls. Glass and acrylic cabochons normally have a foil backing to reflect light. Gemstones and pearls do not.

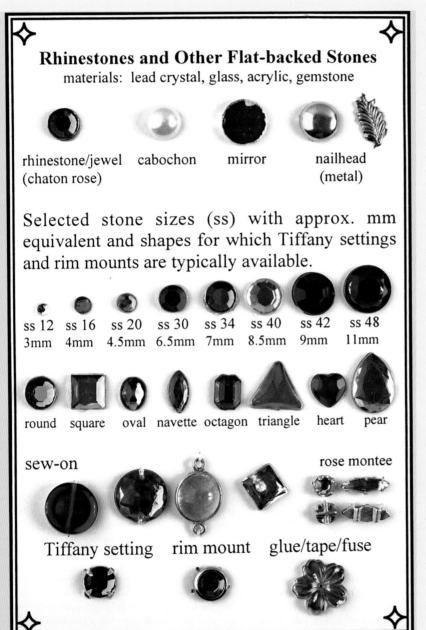

Figure 119

Mounts for rhinestones & cabochons

Both rhinestones and cabochons use the same attachment methods. The method you choose will depend on whether or not the stones you want to use have sewing holes, if you want the extra decoration a mount provides, or if you want a clean unhindered look.

Sew-on mounts

Sew-on rhinestones and cabochons can have the sewing holes in a variety of locations. If a single hole runs the width of the stone or holes are located near the edge, use a simple in-and-out sewing stitch. The stitch may be made with decorative thread or the thread may be covered with seed beads, or purl. Stones with a single hole through the center of the stone, or stones with holes near the edge, can also be sewn into place with a stop bead. Solid acrylic stones can be made into sew-on stones by drilling a hole through them, using a 0.60mm drill bit. This provides a more secure attachment than gluing.

Metal mounts

Metal mounts set stones onto fabric without any sewing. Metal prongs are pushed through the fabric and around the stone to hold it in place. You will use two types of mounts: Tiffany settings and rim mounts.

Stones without mounts

Sometimes, you will glue, tape, or fuse stones in place. (This is considered the least durable way to attach a stone.) Some stones do not have holes and some novelty shapes do not have mounts. Glue, tape, and fusing materials also provide the cleanest look without thread or prongs on the surface. But remember, most of these materials cannot be cleaned.

Apply enough glue so that the glue squeezes out from under the stone and seals all the way around the stone's edges. (See Figure 120) This means the whole stone is captured by the glue and not just the silver backing, which may not be strong enough to support the weight of the stone. It might take a little practice to get just the right amount of glue.

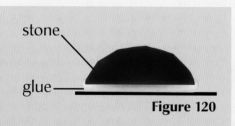

stone

glue

Figure 120

If you want a clean look, yet need fabric to remain flexible, you can glue metal or plastic button backs onto large rhinestones with glue. (See Figure 121) The rhinestone may wobble a bit, but using two or more button backs on one stone will reduce wobbling. Sew the rhinestones onto the fabric through the button backs. You can even use the rhinestones as buttons!

Nailheads

Nailheads are decorative metal tops with prongs on the back. Although they do not have flat backs like rhinestones (the backs are hollow), they serve the same purpose as flat-backed stones and are attached just like rim mounts.

Push the prongs through the fabric from front to back. Then bend the prongs inward to hold the nailhead in place. Use the eraser end of a wooden pencil to bend the prongs over.

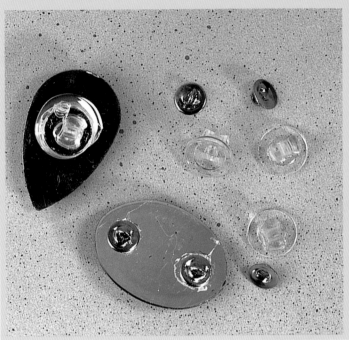

Figure 121

Snagging

The prongs on mounts of rose montée, Tiffany settings, and rim mounts can snag some fabrics. With rim mounts, the piece can be lined to prevent snagging. With rose montée or Tiffany settings, you have to choose fabrics that will not snag or be very careful that the mounts do not rub against fabric.

Settings

A Tiffany setting is almost invisible. It is gold- or silver-toned fabric.

To place a Tiffany setting:
1. Place the setting behind the fabric and push the prongs through to the front.

2. Place the stone within the prongs, and close the prongs over the stone.

A rim mount captures the stone from the front, appearing as a frame around it. Rim mount has the effect of framing the stone and making it appear larger and more decorative. Rim mounts are available in black or gold- or silver-toned.

To place a rim mount:
1. Place the stone in the mount with the face of the stone away from the prongs.

2. Push the prongs through the fabric from the front of the fabric to the back.

3. Fold the prongs in on the back of the fabric.

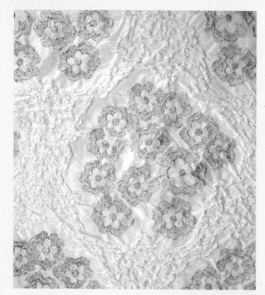
Figure 122

Rose montée

A rose montée is a rhinestone that is prong–mounted in a metal back that has sewing channels in it. Choose a rose montée that has at least two sewing channels to keep the stones from flipping over once they are attached to the fabric.

On a round rose montée, the two channels will form a cross. Because the sewing channels are on the back, a rose montée provides a clean look without the distraction of thread stitches. Variations can be made with montée rhinestones. (See Figures 122 & 123) The crystal rose montée and silver-lined, clear seed beads on silver embroidered silk taffeta is an example.

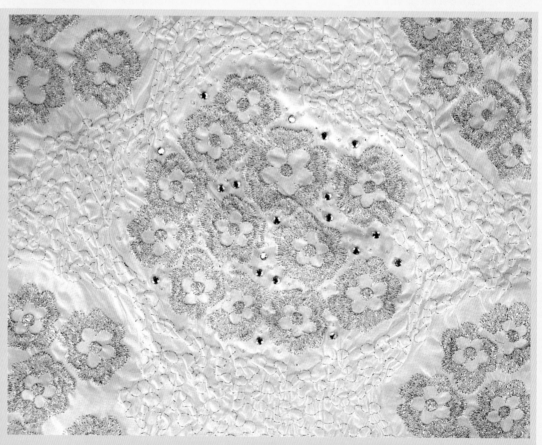
Figure 123

Tape & fusible web

Some new double-sided tapes are available that are strong enough to attach stones to fabric. These tapes should only be used in areas where the fabric is permanently positioned and will not flex. (See Figure 125)

Stones can sometimes be attached with fusible webs. Because fusing requires heat, it can only be used for heat-resistant stones like those made from glass or crystal. Cut a piece of web the size and shape of the base of your stone. Place the stone upside down on a thick wash cloth to hold it in place, and then position web and fabric on top. Follow package instructions to fuse stone to fabric.

Figure 124

Iron-on mounts

A recent innovation is iron-on crystal rhinestones. Individual Swarovski rhinestones have hot-melt glue applied to the back and are available commercially. Swarovski crystal motifs have individual crystals attached to a temporary film in prearranged designs. (See Figure 124) You simply position the motif or individual rhinestone and iron it directly onto your fabric.

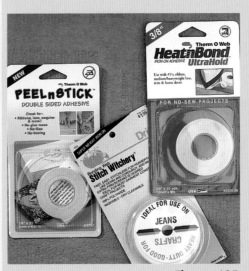

Figure 125

Sizing rhinestones & cabochons

Rhinestones and cabochons are sized using two different systems. The older system uses stone sizes (SS). The newer system is millimeter sizing. You will encounter the millimeter sizing method most frequently, especially for stones larger than 9mm. Round rhinestones are measured by diameter. Cabochons are measured by length and width. Figure 126 lists the possible rhinestone sizes for which mounts are available. Make certain that the stone chosen fits your mount.

Because of rounding errors when converting stones from the SS system to the millimeter system, it is common that stones do not necessarily fit mounts of the same size.

Rhinestones in shapes such as squares, ovals, navettes, octagons (baguettes), hearts, triangles, and pears are also available with mounts.

Novelty shapes, such as stars, flowers, and butterflies are made in acrylic and do not have mounts. These shapes are sized by measuring the length and width in millimeters.

Stone size	Millimeters
12 SS	3mm
16 SS	4mm
20 SS	5mm
30 SS	6.5mm
34 SS	7.5mm
40 SS	8.5 mm
42 SS	9 mm
48 SS	11mm

Figure 126

Figure 127

Shisha

Shisha are small mirrors that have been cut into simple geometric shapes and are used much like rhinestones. Shisha is traditionally used on Indian embroideries where the mirror is held in place with an embroidered thread frame. They also can be attached with rim mounts. Figure 128 on page 91 shows small mirrors added to the existing piece of fabric shown in Figure 127.

Shisha embroidery can be used to attach mirrors to designer fabric such as tambour-embroidered chiffon. (See Figures 129a-h) This piece was also embellished with beaded leaf veins worked in backstitch.

Shisha is available in glass or acrylic. Glass shisha have sharp, unpolished edges and must be handled with care. The edges can be smoothed with a honing stone or sandpaper, making it easier to work with them.

Shisha sizes are limited. They are generally available in the 10mm–30mm range.

Glass shisha are classified as antique, perfect, or rainbow. Antique shisha can be new or old glass. Pieces are called antique because they are produced through the antique method of hand-blowing a glass sheet and then nipping out shapes. In antique shisha, the glass may contain imperfections and bubbles. Perfect shisha is made by machine and free of flaws. Rainbow shisha is also machine-made and has an aurora-borealis coating.

Figure 128

Figure 129a

Figure 129b

Figure 129c

Figure129d

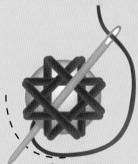

Figure129e

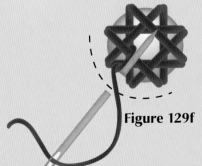

Figure 129f

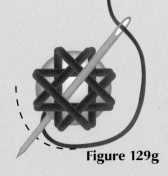

Figure 129g

Figure 129h

91

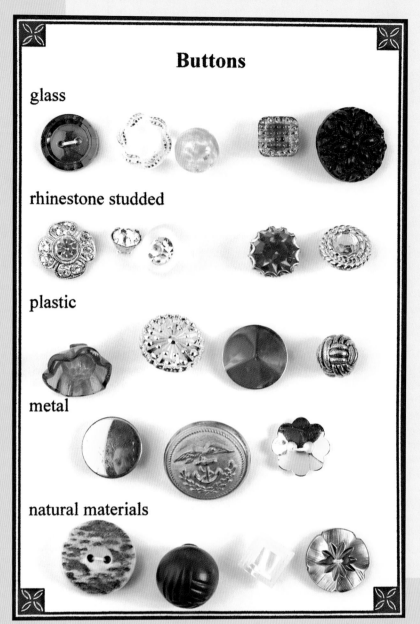

Buttons

glass

rhinestone studded

plastic

metal

natural materials

Figure 130

Buttons

A buttonhole is not necessary when using buttons as part of a trim. Beaded buttons are a quick way to add beads to a project and can be stitched or couched on fabric, or strung over a mold.

Buttons are made from the same materials and use the same techniques as large beads; just the hole placement is different. Buttons made from glass, plastic, metal and natural materials, all coordinate well with beads. (See Figure 130)

Buttons are large and flat, serving much the same function as flat-backed stones. Buttons often become the focal point of a project, because they have a larger surface area and are more heavily decorated than beads.

Figure 131

There are several ways to make designer, beaded buttons. Beads can be glued to a mold, stitched on knit fabric, couched on velvet, or strung over a wood bead.

When stitching beads onto a button mold (See Figures 131 & 132), begin with a commercial nylon button mold covered with knit fabric. Use a lightweight knit such as a T-shirt. The knit is more flexible than woven fabric so it is easier to stitch into when stretched on a mold. Use simple geometric patterns that either radiate from the center or circle the center. If some of the fabric will show, you can use fashion fabric, but it is a little harder to stitch, not being as flexible as knit.

Couching, like stitching, is worked on a mold covered with knit or fashion fabric. In Figure 133, prestrung pearls and pearl purl are couched around a purl flower center.

In Figure 134, the beginning tails of the prestrung beads and twisted cord are flattened and glued under the rhinestone. The beads and cord are then couched in a spiral around the rhinestone.

Figure 132

Figure 133

Figure 134

Figure 135

Beads are strung over molds to make both ball and flat buttons. The principle is to string the maximum number of beads possible in the four cardinal directions and then keep subdividing each quadrant using strings of fewer and fewer beads until the mold is covered. You have to adapt the number of beads needed to the mold. (See Figure 135)

To make a ball button: (See Figure 136a)
1. Use a large wood bead for the mold. The thread that holds the beads goes through the hole of mold on all of the passes except for the initial four groups of beads that define the quadrants.

2. Wrap these groups around the outside of the mold and then hold them in place by passing the thread through the hole and over the + where the wraps cross at the top and bottom of the hole. (See Figure 136b)

To make a flat button: (See Figure 137a)
1. Begin with a fabric covered mold, preferably knit fabric. Use a beading needle because you will need the flexibility to pass the thread between the fabric and mold.

2. Take a tiny stitch at the back edge of the fabric to secure each row.

3. First divide the top into four quadrants by making two long beaded stitches across the center of the mold passing the thread between the mold and fabric to reach the next position. (See Figure 137b)

4. Subdivide each quadrant and fill in using fewer beads with each subdivision. Work each row from edge to edge across the face of the button.

5. Take a stitch under the fabric at the center of the button to pass under beads already in place.

Figure 136a

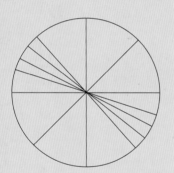

Figure 136b

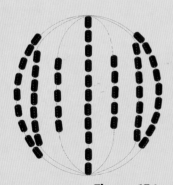

Figure 136c

Figure 137a

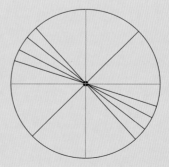

Figure 137b

Beaded buttons

Beading braids, cords & ribbons

Braids and cords can be used in multiple ways in beadwork. Lengths running here and there add flow and movement. The eye will naturally follow from one end of a length to the other. When applied in a circle, the eye stays fixed within that circle. Motifs such as a frog closure draw attention to a single spot.

The distinction between braid, cord, and ribbon is in how each is manufactured. (See Figure 141) Braids are made by intertwining (braiding) fibers. They can be flat or round. Cords are made from one or more strands of fiber that are solid, like leather string, or twisted together, like a miniature rope. Some cords have a solid core with a wrapped, woven, or braided cover. The names of these embellishments are oftentimes confused. For example, soutache and president's braids are really cords.

Small gimp cords stitched into serpentine shapes are also called braids. Do not dwell on names too much, just look at the trim and buy what you like.

Braids and cords are usually made from fiber or synthetic metal. Synthetic metal and fiber are often combined in one trim.

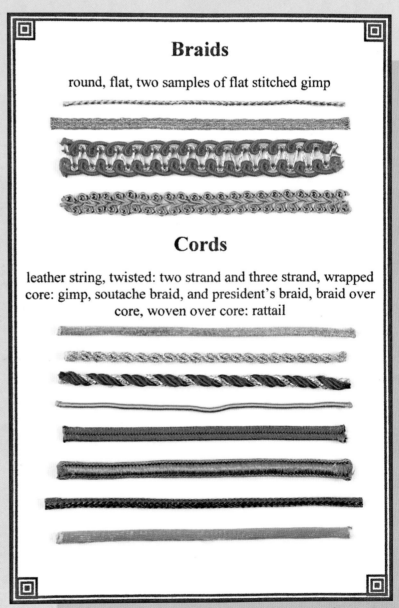

Braids

round, flat, two samples of flat stitched gimp

Cords

leather string, twisted: two strand and three strand, wrapped core: gimp, soutache braid, and president's braid, braid over core, woven over core: rattail

Figure 141

Metal threads

Metal threads are not like sewing thread. They are heavier embellishments made from metal leaf wrapped around a fiber core, metal plate, or coil metal wire. (See Figure 142)

Metal threads are attached to the surface of the fabric like beads. They add an elegant look and rich texture to fashions, home décor, and art embroidery.

Metal threads were originally made from real gold and silver. Today, they are made from alloys or synthetics. Alloys are usually gold or silver colored but can be any color including red, blue, green, and pink.

Synthetic metal threads are made from metalized plastic. Alloys and synthetic metal are cheaper, do not tarnish, and are often more durable than the real metal threads that they imitate.

Short lengths of metal thread are used to imitate seed or bugle beads or to surround beads. Using craft scissors, a piece of metal thread is cut to the desired length. The stitching thread is passed through the hollow core and the length stitched into place. To curve the metal thread into circles or loops, both the beginning and ending stitches are taken in the same place. Metal threads are often worked over padding like the raised and padded lazy stitches.

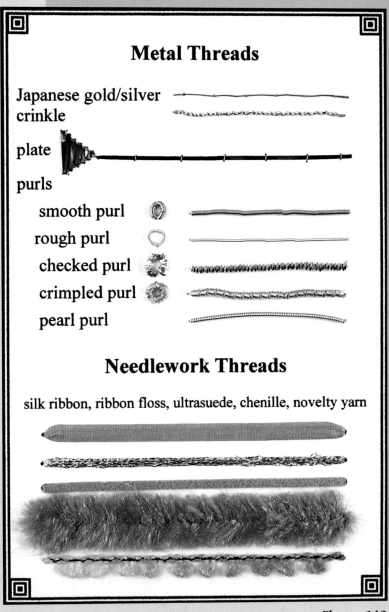

Metal Threads

Japanese gold/silver

crinkle

plate

purls

 smooth purl

 rough purl

 checked purl

 crimpled purl

 pearl purl

Needlework Threads

silk ribbon, ribbon floss, ultrasuede, chenille, novelty yarn

Figure 142

97

Figure 143

Figure 144

Needlework threads

Threads used for needlework, especially larger threads used with needlepoint canvas or in knitting, are usually couched in long lines or spiral designs cutting the thread as little as possible because the ends are difficult to manage neatly. Some needlework threads that are fine enough to pull through fabric, such as embroidery floss and silk ribbon, are used in beading with traditional embroidery stitches.

Needlework threads add color and texture. Consider including threads such as silk ribbon, ribbon floss, ultrasuede strips, chenille, or any of the multitude of novelty yarns available for knitting in your work.

In Figures 143–145, various threads were used to embroider with purl, beads, and sequins. The couching stitch was used to hold long pieces of purl in place. Shorter pieces were held in place by stringing them like beads.

Crazy quilting of long ago and today employ threads of all kinds in fancy intricate stitches, including French knots. The variety of threads used can make the same stitch appear different.

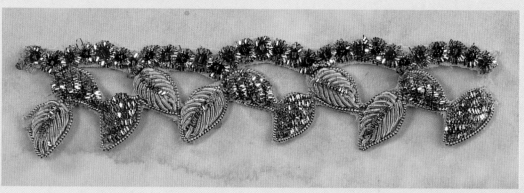

Figure 145

Ribbons

Ribbons are narrow, flat, woven fabrics with two selvages. With some needlework threads, ribbons, and embroidery flosses, you can stitch through the fabric.

Embroidery threads and silk ribbon for silk-ribbon embroidery are designed to hold up under repeated passes through fabric. Other needlework threads and ribbons are not engineered for this treatment and may look abused or fall apart after a few stitches. Test your thread on a swatch and see its performance before beginning your project.

Ribbonwork motifs and trims use beads to focus attention on the ribbonwork. (See Figures 146 & 147) The beads are often placed on functional stitches that either hold the ribbonwork together or attach it to fabric.

Some ribbons are specially made needlework threads that are used in beading.

Figure 146

Figure 147

Figure 148

Applying Decorative Trim

Couching

Braids, cords, metal threads, needlework threads, and ribbons are most frequently applied by couching. The couching stitch is worked for threads in the same manner as for beads, except that the stitches are usually further apart. Spacing depends on the material being couched and whether the pattern line is straight or curved. Couching stitches might be as far as 1" apart along straight pattern lines.

The couching thread may or may not show, depending on the material being stitched and the design. If you do not want the couching stitches to show, use a single strand of sewing thread in a matching color. Keep the stitches evenly spaced and the stitches will blend into the fabric. If you do want the couching thread to show, use a decorative thread or cover the thread with seed beads or purl. The couching stitches then become part of the design.

On the Victorian band in Figure 148, gold cord and prestrung sequins are couched into place. The ribbon is tacked in place with seed beads, heart and rose buttons, and leaf beads. When couching twisted cord, such as the gold twisted cord, you can hide the couching thread by couching only the strand of the cord that is touching the fashion fabric. (See Figure 149)

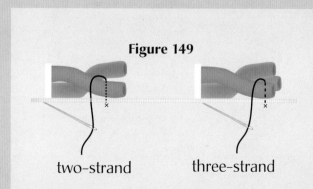

Figure 149

two-strand   three-strand

Finishing the ends

The most challenging aspect of using braids, cords, needlework threads, and ribbons is how to finish the ends. Cut ends seem to have a mind of their own, and that usually means unraveling or fraying. Several methods of finishing ends are used including gluing the end in a bead, tying an overhand knot and fringing the end, toggle knot, inverted end, folded end, Turk's head knot, embroidered end, lazy stitch end, and passing the strands to the back.

Glue end in bead

The first method shown is simply to glue the tail in a bead. (See Figure 150) Choose a bead with a hole large enough to accept the braid or cord. Stitch the bead into place, then glue the end of the braid of cord and push it into the bead hole.

Overhand knot & fringe end

An end can be finished by tying an overhand knot in the end of the braid, cord or ribbon. Fraying the loose end is optional and gives a more decorative appearance.

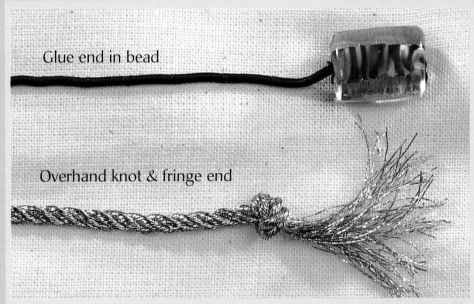

Glue end in bead

Overhand knot & fringe end

Figure 150

Figure 151

Toggle knot

A toggle knot makes a good end when you want a braid or cord to end abruptly. (See Figure 151)

To make a toggle knot:

1. Lay the cord along your index finger from palm to finger tip. (See Figure 152a)

2. Wrap the cord around the tail and your finger five times beginning at your finger tip and wrapping back toward your palm. (See Figure 152b)

3. Slip coil off of your finger holding all of the wraps in place. Pass the tail of the end you were wrapping through the center of the coil in the opposite direction that the beginning tail goes through. (See Figure 152c)

4. Pull on both tails while twisting the wraps to tighten the toggle. Pull hard on the tails to make the toggle as tight as possible. Cut the unwanted end close to the toggle knot. (See Figure 152d)

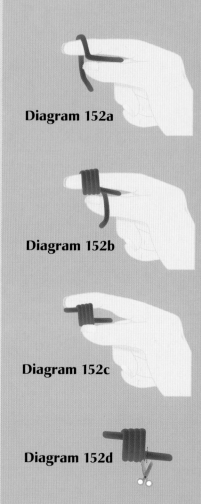

Diagram 152a

Diagram 152b

Diagram 152c

Diagram 152d

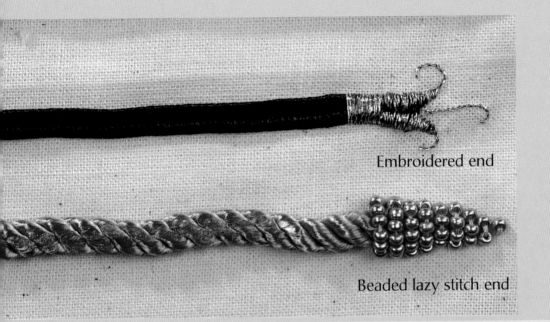

Embroidered end

Beaded lazy stitch end

Figure 153

Embroidered end

An embroidered satin stitch can form an unobtrusive end if worked with thread in a matching color, or can be decorative if worked with contrasting thread. (See Figure 151) The key is to make closely spaced, parallel stitches. For thick braids or cords, thin the end by tapering or removing the core. On twisted cords, cut each strand to a different length to gradually reduce the diameter near the end.

Beaded lazy stitch end

The beaded end is a variation of the padded lazy satin stitch. A decorative cord replaces the upholstery cord and only the end of the cord is covered. For thick braids or cords, thin the end by tapering or removing the core. On twisted cords, cut each strand to a different length to gradually reduce the diameter near the end. Tack the ends down securely with thread before beading.

Figure 154

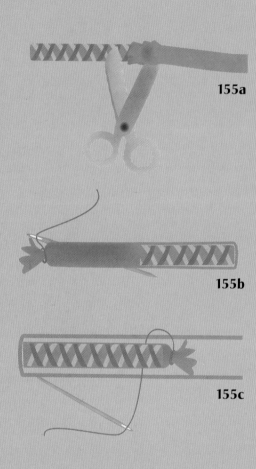

155a

155b

155c

Inverted end

Braids that are made of a core with a braided cover can be finished by inverting the end of the cover. (See Figure 154)

To invert the end:

1. Pull the cover back and cut off 1" of core. (See Figure 155a)

2. Push the cover back into place. With needle and thread, tie the neck of the cover closed tightly near the cut end. (See Figure 155b)

3. Knot the thread but do not cut. Pass the needle through the cover, starting just below the closed end and emerging near the top of the shortened core.

4. Roll the cover between thumb and index finger while pulling down on the thread. The closed end will pull down inside the cover. (See Figure 155c)

5. Knot and cut the thread.

Note: Two inverted ends can be blind stitched together to make a continuous braid design such as a circle.

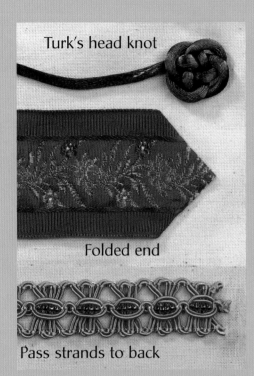

Turk's head knot

Folded end

Pass strands to back

Figure 156

Figure 157

Turk's head knot

For a really decorative end, make a Turk's head knot. (See Figure 156) Photocopy the pattern in Figure 157 reducing or enlarging if necessary. Lay the cord on top of the pattern to weave it. With a little practice, you will be able to weave the knot in your hand without the pattern. Stitch the start tail to the back of the knot, then cut the tail short so it will be covered by the knot when the knot is stitched in place.

Folded end

Ribbons and flat braids can have the end folded under and stitched down.

Pass strands to back

This example has small individual strands of the braid pulled to the back of the fabric. This method is also used for needlework threads.

To pass strands to the back:
1. Unravel about 4" of braid, leaving the tails intact. If the braid is stitched together with chain stitches, knot the chain stitch thread so it will not continue to unravel.

2. Using a large chenille needle, thread one strand of the braid. Push the needle into the fabric and, while still in the fabric, work the shank of the needle back and forth or in a circle to push the fabric weave apart, creating a hole large enough for the strand to pass through. Pull the strand through.

3. Repeat for all of the other strands and threads, creating a different hole for each one.

4. When all are through, knot or couch the strands and threads in place.

Beading on fabric

The first of several factors to consider when designing and executing a beaded project on fabric is weight. Beading fabric affects the drape of the fabric and can exaggerate any stretch the fabric might have. The weight of beads may even distort the weave of the fabric or tear the fabric if too great. On woven fabrics, areas that hang on the bias will stretch much more than adjacent areas that are on the straight grain. You may need to limit a bead design to areas of a piece that are on the straight grain only or at least reduce the number of beads in bias areas. Knits do not have a bias but stretch much more in the horizontal direction than in the vertical direction and this can cause similar draping problems. Remember, weight matters!

Second, consider how your project will be used when placing your design. For beaded fashions, you do not want to sit on bulky beads. Even beads on the back of a garment can poke when sitting in a chair. If you lean on the beaded pillows on your sofa, limit beads to pillow edges. You do not want the beads from the pillow poking you either.

Third, take shrinkage into account. Fabric shrinks from two sources in beading, natural shrinkage of fabric when cleaned and shrinkage from tension on the beading thread. Preshrink fabric if you ever intend to clean it.

Use an embroidery frame to minimize fabric shrinkage caused by beading. Be certain to leave wide margins around large or heavily beaded pieces so the pattern for the fabric piece can be remarked after beading is completed.

Overall designs must be beaded before the pieces are cut from the fabric. Small areas of beading, such as fringes and trims, can be applied after the garment is completed.

Appliqués are stitched separately from a project. This way, fabric shrinkage due to tension on the beading thread is limited to the appliqué backing.

Fourth, beadwork needs a lot of support. Underline the fashion fabric with a second layer of firmly woven fabric if necessary. Choose garment patterns that use interfacings.

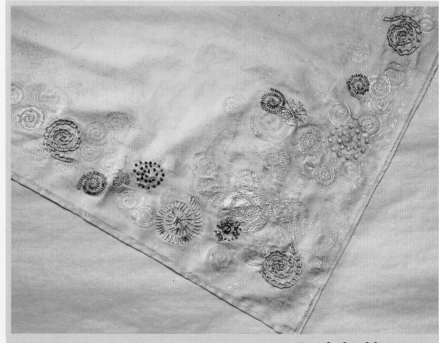

Beaded table runner
Owned by Jo Packham

Woven fabrics

You can bead woven fabrics as sheer as organdy and as heavy as upholstery. Below are tips to help you get good results with a variety of woven fabrics.

• Make certain the beading pattern is on the straight grain of the fabric. If it is off even a little, beads will cause the slight bias to stretch and the garment will never hang straight.

• If beads on a garment make one section heavier than another (for instance, beading on the front of a vest but not the back), the garment may rotate on the body. Add dressmaker's weights to balance the weight.

• When beading on sheer fabric such as chiffon (See Figure 158) space beads widely apart to prevent the fabric from tearing.

• Line your beadwork. Even a pillow top should be lined. Inserting the pillow form can snag the underlying threads.

Figure 158

• For sheer fabrics that need underlining or interfacing to support the beadwork, use a second or even third layer of the fashion fabric. This maintains the sheer look while adding the necessary support.

• Use woven interfacings. Fusible interfacings do not work well with beads.

• On napped fabrics, use felt under beaded motifs to keep small beads from sinking into the fabric.

• To maintain a straighter hem, let beaded garments hang for several days before hemming.

Knit fabrics

Knits can be successfully beaded, however, the considerations in design planning are different than those for woven fabrics. Knits stretch more in a horizontal direction than in the vertical direction. You should consider the direction of stitching lines, as well as the total weight of the beads.

For open knits or heavily beaded knits, you need to underline the knit with a woven fabric. Open knits with large holes resulting from oversized knitting needles need the underlining because the beads tend to pull through the fabric.

Heavily beaded knits need the underlining to keep the knit from stretching out of shape from the weight of the beads. The underlining will reduce or eliminate the stretch so you will have to treat the fabric sandwich as a woven fabric.

To maintain overall stretch, bead in small individual motifs. Each motif is stitched into place, then the thread is knotted off and cut. (See Figure 159) The fabric behind the motif will not stretch due to the tension on the stitching threads but the fabric between motifs is free to stretch as usual. On more expensive garments, a small piece of woven interfacing is placed behind each motif to support the beads. If the beadwork is solid, interfacing could be placed under the motif as for a padded satin stitch.

Knits are beaded in hand without a frame. Be careful to neither pull the stitching thread so tightly that the knit puckers, nor leave it so loose that the beads droop away from the fabric.

Some types of stitches work better than others with knits. The lazy stitch is more flexible than other stitches and is, therefore, a good choice.

Tiny seed beads tend to get buried in knit, so bugle beads work better. Heavy beads will pull on the fabric, so avoid them.

When working with sequins and beads on knit fabric, create widely spaced motifs that are individually tied off to maintain the knit's stretch.

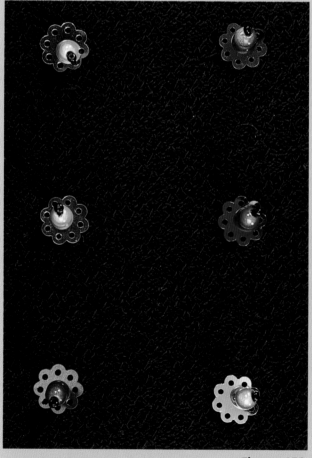

Figure 159

You can maintain the stretch in a beaded knit garment with careful planning. If you bead in a vertical direction, you will avoid many of the problems of stitching knits. Knits stretch much less in a vertical direction than they do in a horizontal one, sometimes not at all. When beading a vertical direction, you can bead in narrow bands and ignore the stretch.

The beads in the cable in Figure 160 are attached in short vertical sections. Within each section, the beads are attached in groups of three. (See Figure 161)

To maintain stretch when beading in a horizontal direction, you must use a duplicate stitch to attach the beads. The duplicate stitch follows the yarn path horizontally across a row. Beads are added to stitches as necessary, following a charted pattern. Use beads about the same length as the knit stitch is tall. Simple geometric designs work best.

Ideally you can use a strand of the same yarn that was used to knit the fabric to work the duplicate stitch. But this is not always the case. If you want to bead on a purchased knit garment and no extra yarn is available, a great choice is to use a decorative yarn, such as a metallic yarn or a fine knitting yarn. If you purchased knitted yardage, you can buy a little extra and unravel a few rows to give you matching yarn to work with.

When working the duplicate stitch on sweater knits made of sport weight or worsted weight yarns, you will find the yarn is too thick to go through the beads. Reduce the yarn to a 1-ply. A single ply of yarn has very little strength, however, so you can either twist it to make it stronger before stitching, or double it back on itself to make a 2-ply strand.

Figure 160

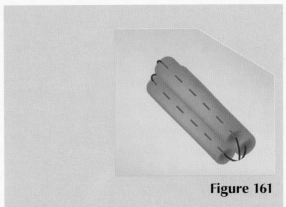

Figure 161

Figure 162

Beads attached with duplicate stitches to maintain horizontal stretch. Stitched with one ply of a three-ply yarn. The single ply was twisted tightly after separating it from the yarn to strengthen it. (See Figures 162 & 163)

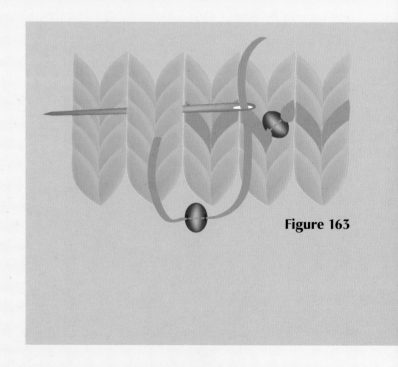

Figure 163

Figure 164

Beading on lace & net

Beads make an effective addition to lace and net, adding sparkle and color. Color can be a great addition to laces and nets that are only available in white or ecru. Lace appliqués, lace trim, and lace yardage can all be beaded. (See Figures 164 & 165) Re-embroidered laces are ideal. Bead in the structurally strongest part of the pattern, usually the area with the most threads. Use lightweight sequins on weaker areas. Beading usually echos some part of the lace design so a pattern is not necessary.

Figure 165

"Net" refers to bobbin net, also called tulle. It does not refer to nylon net, which is not strong enough for beading. It has a hexagonal mesh made from silk or cotton. In Figure 166 seed beads and ribbon roses are stitched onto cotton tulle. Cotton tulle comes in white and can be dyed any color.

Beads must be larger than the holes in the net or the beads will slip through to the back of the net. Net is commonly available in 14 and 18 meshes to the inch. The smallest beads you can use are 11° with 14-count mesh and 13° with 18-count mesh.

Beads stitched on net seem to float in the air. When used on a veil, beads form a halo. When used as an overlay, beads seem to dance. It is important to keep the weight down when beading on net. Beading is usually done in small, widely spaced motifs. (If you are beading a veil, you want the wearer to be able to see out between the motif.) Lightweight materials such as sequins and ribbon roses can be used to reduce weight.

Because of the net's structure, beading on net is different from beading on other fabrics. Use a single strand of thread in a color to match the net. You do not want the thread to be visible or to be stronger than the threads that make up the net. If a bead gets caught, you want the stitching thread to break, not the mesh.

Each seed bead should sit in a separate hexagonal mesh. There are two primary ways to stitch seed beads on net and lace. One stitch is used for beading vertical rows and another for beading horizontal rows.

You can turn the net in any direction you like so that it is easy to work the stitches. Just remember that there are two different stitches used for seed beads. Look at the mesh pattern and decide which is the proper stitch to use.

Larger beads and regular beading stitches can be used on net. Bugle beads work well. Use either of the net stitches or a running or backstitch. Stitches such as a lazy stitch work well on net also.

Figure 166

Beading in vertical rows

For beading vertical rows (See Figure 167):

1. Pass the needle behind the horizontal bar that separates two meshes from right to left (reverse for lefties).

2. Pick up a bead, and pass the needle behind the next horizontal bar one row up. In this stitch, the needle passes behind two diagonal bars of the mesh with each stitch.

3. Attach the stitching thread to the mesh, using a slip knot around a bar of the mesh or just tie the stitching thread to a bar.

4. To end, tie the stitching thread to a bar.

5. To move across unbeaded areas without breaking the thread, weave the thread through the bars of the mesh.

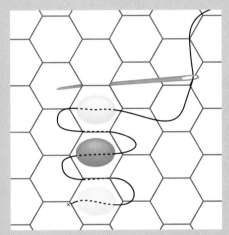

Figure 167

Beading in horizontal rows

For beading horizontal rows (See Figure 168):

1. Attach the stitching thread to the mesh, using a slip knot around a bar of the mesh or just tie the stitching thread to a bar.

2. Pass the needle from top to bottom behind one horizontal bar.

3. Pick up a bead, skip one full hexagon, and pass the needle behind the next horizontal bar. In this stitch, the needle passes behind one horizontal bar of the mesh with each stitch.

4. To end, tie the stitching thread to a bar.

5. To move across unbeaded areas without breaking the thread, weave the thread through the bars of the mesh.

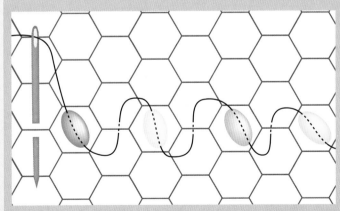

Figure 168

Beading on purchased trims

If you are not up to beading a whole garment, pillow top, or other large item, try beading a trim and attaching that to a larger project. The trim itself provides all of the guidelines you need for stitching so you do not have to mark the pattern either. An added advantage to beading on trims is that any shrinkage due to beading occurs in the trim before it is applied to your project. Additionally, the trim can be removed should it become necessary to clean the item.

The examples in Figure 169 show several easy-to-bead patterns using the trim itself as the beading guide.

The blue ribbon with soutache-braid diamonds has a bead stitched in the center of each diamond.

The white ribbon with dots has a matching bead stitched on top of each dot.

The ribs in the red and the red and white grosgrain ribbons are used to keep the beads straight and evenly spaced.

A braid made of three strands of soutache braid is highlighted with seed beads stitched in the center ditch of each strand where exposed.

Figure 169

Figure 170

Figure 171

Figure 172

Making appliqués on nylon organdy

If you want to make a beaded trim separate from your project and do not want the backing to show as it does with the trims in the previous section, you can make an appliqué by doing the beadwork on nylon organdy in an embroidery frame. Nylon organdy is a strong, stiff, sheer fabric available in several colors. If you cannot find nylon organdy, you can use two layers of polyester organdy.

Patterns are transferred and beads are sewn onto nylon organdy in the same manner as any other sheer fabric. Nylon organdy will stand up to fairly dense, heavy beadwork. The real difference comes in how the beadwork is handled when beading is complete.

To apply appliqué:

1. Turn the frame with the beadwork over and spread a layer of fabric glue over the entire back of the appliqué. (See Figure 170)

Note: This adheres all of the stitching threads to the nylon organdy, increasing durability and keeping the beads from being lost if the stitching thread is accidentally cut when excess organdy is trimmed.

2. After the glue dries, remove the appliqué from the embroidery frame and trim the excess organdy.

3. If you need a flexible appliqué, glue only around the edges where the organdy will be trimmed, as done in the choker in Figure 171.

4. If the appliqué has straight edges, you can eliminate the gluing step and trim the organdy 1" from the stitching. (See Figure 172) Fold the organdy edges under the appliqué as for a hem. You can bead the fold with a small picot edge if desired.

Figure 173

Beading trims

Bead strings can be used effectively as trims on fabrics.
(See Figure 173) These are strung separately, then couched
onto the fabric. Most bead strings were originally designed
as necklaces or bracelets; however, some were designed
specifically as fabric trims. These trims could also be attached
as fringes. As with beading on purchased trims, these strung
trims can be removed when a project is cleaned.

Figure 175

Figure 176

The colorful beads in Figure 174 were strung in a line (See Figure 176) then couched on the fabric incorporating a curve where desired.

The beading in Figure 175 was made to be worn as a choker. Sets of seed beads are joined creating circles. (See Figure 177)

Figure 177

Figure 174

117

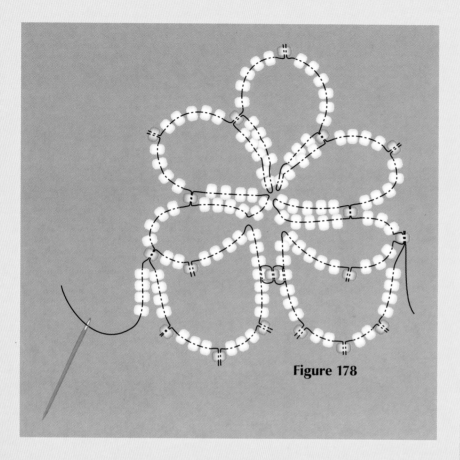

Figure 178

The tatting in Figure 179 was originally made to use as a fabric trim. Blue
and white beads were strung using a
tatting pattern. The trim was then
couched flat onto fabric. (See Figure
178) The trim could also serve as fringe
when attached to the edge of fabric
with a running stitch.

Figure 179

Fagotting

Fagotting is short, repeated lengths of strung beads placed between two pieces of fabric, braid, or ribbon. (See Figure 182) Be certain to use strong thread.

Fagotting can be worked between lengths of soutache braid (See Figure 180) or ribbon. (See Figure 181) It functions as a decorative trim, seam, or insertion. Fagotting makes ideal straps for summer tops and dresses. It looks great on purse handles, and it can form eye-catching seams.

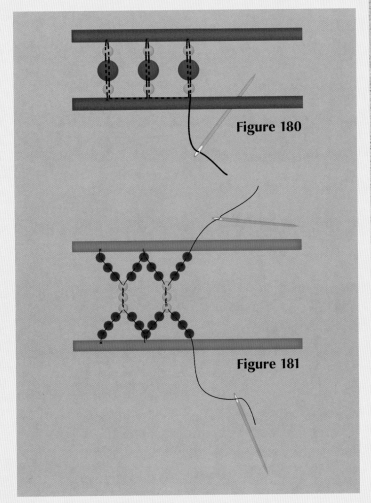

Figure 180

Figure 181

Figure 182

Figure 183

Tassels

Tassels are like exclamation points for fabrics. (See Figure 183) Whenever you see a tassel, the eye takes notice. Beaded tassels are heavy so they must be placed in a structurally strong or reinforced area of fabric. Tassels are ideal on the ends of shawls where the added weight helps hold the shawl in place.

Tassels can have a beaded head, beaded neck, and/or beaded skirt. For a fast tassel, roll fringe that has been beaded on a header into a spiral around a thick cord like the right tassel in Figure 183. Most beaded tassels are made using bead–stringing techniques, like the center two. The left tassel combines braidwork and beadwork.

Entire books have been written on beaded tassels. You can refer to one of them for more ideas.

Figure 184

Rolled fringe tassel

(See Figure 184)
Beaded fringe on a header, 12"
Rattail cord, 6"
Scissors
Sewing thread
Sharp needle

1. Tie ends of rattail cord together.

2. Wrap header of beaded fringe around rat-tail cord above the knot, stitching while wrapping.

3. Fold under last ½" of header and stitch down firmly.

Victorian tassel

(See Figure 185)
Beading needle, #10
Beads:
    decorative beads, 4mm (17); 6mm (4)
    flower cup (trumpet) bead (1)
    seed beads, 11° (10 grams)
Hypo cement
Quilting thread to match bead color
Scissors
Wax, if using quilting thread

Figure 185

1. Start with 3' of thread doubled. If using quilting thread, wax thread.

2. Tie one seed bead 3" from end of thread. String on one 6mm decorative bead and 36 seed beads. Skip last seed bead and return through other 35 seed beads and decorative bead.

3. Knot thread around seed bead that has the thread end tied around it. Go down through decorative bead.

4. Make five more strands of seed beads repeating method above.

5. Tie thread to thread tail with a square knot.

6. Seal knot with hypo cement but do not cut thread.

7. String the following sequence of beads: 2 seed beads, 4mm decorative bead, 3 seed beads, 4mm decorative beads, 3 seed beads, 4mm decorative bead, 3 seed beads, 4mm decorative bead, 7 seed beads. Leave 8" tail and cut thread.

8. Make three more dangles.

9. With overhand knot, tie all four dangles together positioning knot so it touches top seed bead on each dangle. Thread on flower cup, 4mm decorative bead, and 20 seed beads.

10. Pass thread through 4mm decorative bead and flower cup again. Work threads through one at a time if necessary.

11. Tie off threads under flower cup, seal knots with hypo cement, and cut threads close.

Studio bead tassel

(See Figure 186)
Beading needle, #10
Beads:
    cathedral: small (5), large (1)
    freshwater pearls (27)
    gold, 6mm (2)
    seed (325)
    studio, large (1)
Hypo cement
Quilting thread to match bead color
Scissors
Wax if using quilting thread

1. Start with 2' of doubled thread. If using quilting thread, wax thread.

2. String on 1 pearl and 10 seed beads three times, 1 small cathedral bead, 10 seed beads, and 1 pearl two times, and 10 seed beads.

3. Pass the needle and thread back through the first pearl. Remove the needle, but do not cut thread tails.

4. Make five loops. Tie loops together so the top of each pearl touches the knot.

5. Seal the knot with hypo cement. Cut one tail off of each loop, leaving five thread tails. String gold bead, studio bead, gold bead, pearl, large cathedral bead, pearl, and 25 seed beads onto all five thread tails. Work threads through one at a time if necessary.

6. Skip seed beads just strung and pass tails back through the next four beads. Tie off between gold bead and studio bead (or you can tie one tail off between each two adjacent beads above the studio bead).

7. Seal knots with hypo cement and cut threads close.

Figure 186

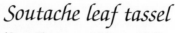

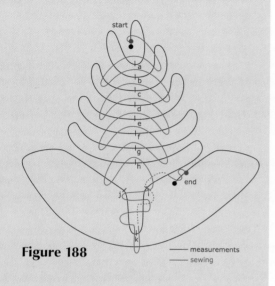

Figure 188

— measurements
— sewing

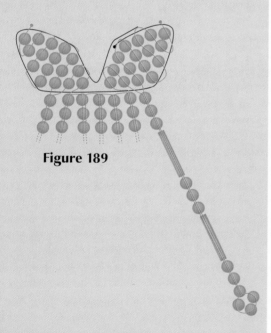

Figure 189

Figure 187

Soutache leaf tassel

(See Figures 188 & 189)
Beads:
    bugle beads, #5 (16)
    seed (168)
Needles:
    beading
    fine sewing
Quilting thread
Scissors
Soutache braid, 13¼"

1. Sew the leaf shape first. Using single-strand quilting thread, bind ends of soutache braid with thread to keep braid from unraveling.

2. Begin at start and sew through two layers of soutache as braid is folded back and forth across center according to the measurements below and Figure 186. Thread will straighten out as it is pulled taut and braid will curve upward. Sew in the center dip of the soutache braid.

Measurements:
start, 1" (a), 1" (b), 1" (c), 1¹⁄₁₆" (d), 1¹⁄₁₆" (e), 1⅛" (f), 1⅛" (g), 1³⁄₁₆" (h), 1³⁄₁₆" (h), ¾" (j), 1½" (k), 1¼", end

3. Bead inside leaves and add dangles. (See Figure 187)

4. Sew through the soutache braid along the center dip. Backstitch beads along vein.

5. Couch completed leaf into place.

Glossary

Aught–a zero

Braid–made by intertwining fibers

Bugle bead–long tubular bead made from glass cane with a round or hexagonal cross section, the same cane used for seed beads

Cabochon–round or oval stone with a smooth, rounded top

Charlotte–a size 13° true-cut bead

Cord–one or more tightly twisted strands of fiber that are solid

Couching–stitching used to attach prestrung beads or embellishments onto fabric

Dangle–beads attached at one end of a strand instead of in the center

Drop bead–a seed bead with an off-center hole

Druk–round, glass beads

Faceted bead–seed bead with multiple flat faces

Fagotting–short repeating lengths of strung beads placed between two pieces of fabric, braid, or ribbon

Fancy bead–large decorative bead used for accent

Fiber optic bead–made of fused glass strands and resembling a cat's eye

Fringe–long, individual dangles stitched next to each other in a line

Glass cane–long tubes of glass

Hank–ten or twelve lengths of prestrung beads tied together

Maco tube–tiny glass tubular bead

Metal threads–heavy embellishment made from metal leaf wrapped around fiber core, metal plate, or coiled metal wire

Mount–metal frame with points that are pushed through fabric and bent over to secure a rhinestone

Nailhead–flat or dome-shaped metal ornament to mimic bead

Net–fringe where the dangles are attached to their neighbors to add stability

Opaque–a solid color that you cannot see through

Organdy–strong, stiff sheer fabric

Paillette–a sequin with the hole at one edge so it can hang freely

Purl–a fine wire coiled on a mandrel (metal rod) and used for beading

Pick stitch–passing the needle from the back through the fold or edge of fabric catching just a few threads of the fabric

Picot edge–beaded fringe where ends are tied together

Pounce pad–powdered chalk in a sock or bag used to transfer pattern lines

Prick-and-pounce–marking method using chalk

Pricking–piercing holes along a pattern line

Rhinestone–bead with faceted front and flat back, which has a foil coating applied to reflect light

Ribbon–narrow, flat, woven fabric with two selvages

Rocailles–French term for seed beads

Rose montée–a rhinestone that is prong-mounted in a metal back that has sewing channels in it

Sashiko–Japanese pattern composed of long lines of running stitches that intersect at various angles

Seed bead–small, donut-shaped glass bead

Sequin–traditionally flat metal circle with a single hole in the center

Shisha–small round, square, triangular or diamond-shaped mirrors

Slate frame–consists of two pairs of stretcher bars

Tatting–a fine lace made by looping and knotting thread

Tosca–bead with a square hole and silver lining

Translucent–a diffused color allowing light through the center

Transparent–clear or colored glass that is easy to see through

True-cut bead–a seed bead with one flat face

Tulle–bobbin net or net is a hexagonal mesh made from silk or cotton

Vermicelli–a continuous, wandering line of stitched beads

References

Benson, Ann, 1993, *Beadweaving*, Sterling Publishing Co., New York, NY.

Conlon, Jane, 1999, *Fine Embellishment Techniques*, Taunton Press, Newtown, CT.

Eha, Nancy, 1997/1999, *Off The Beadin' Path*, Creative Visions Press, St. Paul, MN.

Forrington, Sandy, *Tatted Bead Lace, Bead & Button*, Feb 1995, p. 23-25.

Pina, Leslie, et al., 1999, *Beads in Fashion 1900-2000*, Schiffer Publishing Ltd., Atglen, PA.

Thompson, Angela, *Embroidery with Beads*, 1987/1997, Lacis, Berkeley, CA.

White, Mary, 1904/1972, *How to Do Beadwork*, Dover Publications, Inc., New York, NY.

Acknowledgments

The author would like to thank the following businesses for product:

General Bead (beads/sequins/rhinestones)
317 National City Blvd. National City, CA 91950
(619) 336-0100
genbead.com

Kreinik (metallic threads/wholesale only)
3106 Lord Baltimore Drive, Suite 101
Baltimore, MD 21244
kreinik.com

Lacis (cotton tulle)
2982 Adeline Berkeley, CA 94703
(510) 843-7290
lacis.com

Ornamental Resources (beads)
1427 Miner St. PO Box 3010
Idaho Springs, CO 80452
(303) 567-2222
ornabead.com

Rajmahal
1 Anderson Street
Bendigo, Victoria,
Australia 3550
(61) 03 54417787
rajmahal.com.au

Rhinestone Guy (rhinestones)
1201 E. Chestnut, Suite B
Santa Ana, CA 92701
(714) 547-1700
rhinestoneguy.com

Rings and Things (beads)
PO Box 450 Spokane, WA 99210-0450
(509) 624-8565
rings-things.com

Treadleart (shisha mirrors)
25834 Narbonne Ave. Lomita, CA 90717
(310) 534-5122
treadleart.com

US source (metallic threads)
Jdr-be.com

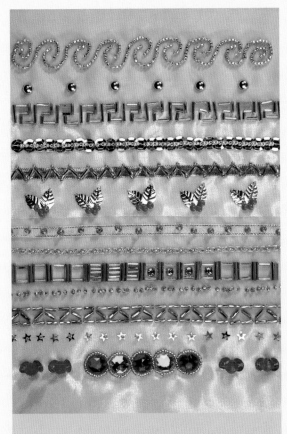

Conversion chart

inches	mm	cm
⅛	3	0.3
¼	6	0.6
⅜	10	1.0
½	13	1.3
⅝	16	1.6
¾	19	1.9
⅞	22	2.2
1	25	2.5
1¼	32	3.2
1½	38	3.8
1¾	44	4.4
2	51	5.1
3	76	7.6
4	102	10.2
5	127	12.7

About the author

Nancy Nehring is a nationally recognized author, teacher and designer in the needle arts field. She is the author of four other books: *50 Heirloom Buttons to Make, The Lacy Knitting of Mary Schiffmann, Ribbon Trims,* and *The Big Book of Tassels.*

Numerous needle art magazines including *Threads, PieceWork,* and *BeadWork* have carried her work. She has designed for DMC, Donna Karan, and Dynamic Resources Group among others. She lectures and teaches locally, regionally and nationally including Embroiderers' Guild of America Seminar, Crochet Guild of America Chain Link, and Stitches.

Although Nancy has sewn since she was 11 or 12 years old, she didn't become a bead aficionado until she took a college course in scientific glassblowing (Nancy has a BS in chemistry and an MA in Natural Science). Her workstation was the only one to have little glass beads rolling around among the test tubes she made. The test tubes were good enough for an A and the beads found their way home and onto her clothing designs.

Nancy lives in Sunnyvale, CA, with her husband, three children, cat, iguana, cockatiel, bunny, chicken, and goldfish. Missing beads surface in the possession of one of the two girls or the cat.

Index